Religions in World- and Global History

Hans-Heinrich Nolte

Religions in World- and Global History

A View from the German-language Discussion

Bibliographic Information published by the Deutsche Nationalbibliothek
The Deutsche Nationalbibliothek lists this publication in the Deutsche Nationalbibliografie; detailed bibliographic data is available in the internet at http://dnb.d-nb.de.

ISBN 978-3-631-67065-1 (Print)
E-ISBN 978-3-653-06291-5 (E-Book)
DOI 10.3726/978-3-653-06291-5

© Peter Lang GmbH
Internationaler Verlag der Wissenschaften
Frankfurt am Main 2015
All rights reserved.
Peter Lang Edition is an Imprint of Peter Lang GmbH.

Peter Lang – Frankfurt am Main · Bern · Bruxelles ·
New York · Oxford · Warszawa · Wien

All parts of this publication are protected by copyright. Any utilisation outside the strict limits of the copyright law, without the permission of the publisher, is forbidden and liable to prosecution. This applies in particular to reproductions, translations, microfilming, and storage and processing in electronic retrieval systems.

This publication has been peer reviewed.

www.peterlang.com

Abstract

The author is arguing, that religious history is underestimated in its importance for World- and Global history. He sketches reasons in methods: history of religions quite often is an established subdiscipline with convincing traditions in research. Also he sketches substantive reasons: for reconstructing the past adequately, historians are in need of academically controlled data about the beliefs of the people they are dealing with. Ten examples are offered – from the history of the medieval Church and early modern Protestantism, Russian Old-Believers and the Orthodox Church of the Empire, from Islam as fundamentalist opposition to Russian expansion and Christian democracy as a conservative Catholic movement stabilizing democracy in Germany and Italy, from secularization as European "Sonderweg" and religious backgrounds of the renewed East-West confrontation, towards – last but not least – the new creed Orisha, which became global with its centre in Africa. The examples show, that developments in religion have far reaching consequences in general history – in the change from Empire to the system of European nations, in establishing social discipline as part of capitalist societies, in attempts of semi-peripheral states to get a place in the European World-System, in defence of Muslim societies on the peripheries and in postcolonial Africa.

Contents

I   General remarks and definitions 9

     I.1   World and Global History – an inter-disciplinary project 9

     I.2   World and Global History – on concepts 16

     I.3   Religions and civilizations 22

II   Case-Studies 29

     II.1   Some famous ones 29

     II.2   Catholic Church and European World System in the 13th century 30

     II.3   Protestantism and nation-states in the 16th cy. "Konfessionsbildung" and social discipline 34

     II.4   "Old belief" as protest against the modernising tendency of the Russian Orthodox Church in the 17th century 41

     II.5   The Russian Orthodox Church serving enlightened absolutism in the 18th century and yet loosing the Patriarchy and monasteries 44

     II.6   Islam as an anti-colonial movement in the Caucasus in the 19th century 47

     II.7   Christian Democracy as European variant for politics in the 20th century 50

     II.8   Secularisation as European "Sonderweg" 53

	II.9	The role of religions in the developing East-West-conflict in Europe 57
	II.10	Orisha 62

III	Conclusions for Histories of the World and of the World-System 65

I General remarks and definitions

I.1 World and Global History – an inter-disciplinary project

This essay is written in the conviction, that World- and Global-History is an interdisciplinary project of a couple of humanities – history, economics, political science, sociology, psychology and others.[1] The special contribution of my field history to this alliance is finding and reading sources in the original languages.[2] My argument runs, that religious history should be included in these meetings of faculties, that this specialty of the sciences about mankind should be asked for cooperation in the task.

To make it easier to see my colours in this attempt, let me name some of the older colleagues, of whom I read texts, and cite some of the younger colleagues, with whom I have learned. In history some of the older colleagues are Leopold von Ranke, Jakob Burckhardt, Karl Lamprecht, Fernand Braudel.[3] In eco-

---

1 My attempt: Hans-Heinrich Nolte: *Weltgeschichte. Imperien, Religionen und Systeme*, 15.–19. Jahrhundert, Wien: Boehlau 2005 (hereafter Nolte *Weltgeschichte 1*); The same: *Weltgeschichte des 20. Jahrhunderts*, Wien: Boehlau 2009 (hereafter Nolte, *Weltgeschichte 2*).

2 Hans-Heinrich Nolte: *Geschichte Russlands*, ³Stuttgart: Reclams Universalbibliothek Nr. 18960, 2012 (hereafter Nolte *Russland*); see also Hans-Heinrich Nolte, Bernhard Schalhorn, Bernd Bonwetsch, Hg.: *Quellen zur Geschichte Russlands*, Stuttgart = Reclams Universalbibliothek 19269, 2014 (hereafter *Quellenbuch*)

3 Ernst Schulin Hg.: *Universalgeschichte* = Neue Wissenschaftliche Bibliothek 72, Köln 1974: Kiepenheuer & Witsch; Paul Kennedy: *The Rise and Fall of the Great Powers*, New York 1989: Vintage;

nomics I read Adam Smith and Karl Marx.[4] In political science Ernst-Otto Czempiel, Samuel Huntington[5] and again friends and colleagues from Hannover.[6] In sociology Max Weber, Tomas Masaryk, Eric Wolf, Norbert Elias and Immanuel Wallerstein.[7] In psychology Sigmund Freud and Peter R. Hofstätter

---

J. R. McNeill, William H. McNeill: *The Human Web. A Bird's Eye View of World History*, New York 2003: Norton; Jürgen Osterhammel: *Die Verwandlung der Welt*, München 2009: Beck; Matthias Middell Hg.: *Die Verwandlung der Weltgeschichtsschreibung* = Comparativ 20.6 (2010).

4 Bouda Etemad, Jean Batou, Thomas David Hg.: *Towards an international economic and social history*, Essays in honour of Paul Bairoch, Genf 1995: Passé Présent; Ronald Findlay, Kevin O'Rourke: *Power and Plenty*, Princeton 2007: Princeton UP; Angus Maddison: *Contours of the World Economy*, Oxford 2007: Oxford UP.

5 See now Peter Nitschke Hg.: *Der Prozess der Zivilisationen*, Berlin 2014: Frank & Thimme.

6 Bernhard Blanke, Enver Sopjani, Wolfram Lamping Hg.: Die politischen Systeme der Staaten des ehemaligen Jugoslawien, Wiesbaden, erscheint 2015: VS-Verlag; Rolf Pohl, Joachim Perels Hg.: *Normalität der NS-Täter?* = Schriftenreihe des Fritz Bauer Institutes 27, Hannover 2011: Offizin; Wolfgang Jüttner, Oskar Negt, Heinz Thörmer Hg.: *Leitlinien politischen Handelns*, Rolf Wernstedt zum 65., Hannover 2005: Offizin; Gert Schäfer: Gewalt, *Ideologie und Bürokratismus. Das Scheitern eines Jahrhundertexperiments*, Mainz 1994: decaton; Bernhard Blanke, Ulrich Jürgens, Hans Kastendiek Hg.: *Kritik der Politischen Wissenschaft* 2 Bde. Frankfurt 1975: Campus.

7 Hans-Peter Waldhoff, Dursun Tan, Elçin Kürşat-Ahlers Hg.: *Brücken zwischen Zivilisationen*, Frankfurt 1997: IKO; Peter R. Gleichmann: *Soziologie als Synthese*, Hg. Hans-Peter Waldhoff = Figurationen 7, Wiesbaden 2006 (hereafter Gleichmann *Soziologie*).

on psychology of groups.[8] Already now that is an extensive program. Some world-historians argue, that Wallerstein should be excluded, others are not reading psychology any more. Obviously the quantity of the texts is enormous. It is impossible to read "all Marx" and "all Weber" in addition to work in an archive. Therefore one may only read some of their works, following transmitted selections of importance. Despite the obvious arguments against enlarging quantity still further my proposal is, to add religious studies – not theology of a certain religion, but "Religionswissenschaft"[9] – to the program. Up to now history of religions did not play a sufficient role in the contexts of world- or global history within German-language historiography.[10]

---

8 Hans-Peter Waldhoff, Christine Morgenroth, Angela Moré, Michael Kopel Hg.: *Wo denken wir hin? Lebensthemen, Zivilisationspozesse, demokratische Verantwortung*, Gießen 2015: Psychosozial-Verlag.
9 Peter Antes: *Grundriss der Religionsgeschichte: Von der Prähistorie bis zur Gegenwart*, Stuttgart 2006: Kohlhammer; Johann Figl Hg.: *Handbuch Religionswissenschaft. Religionen und ihre zentralen Themen* Darmstadt 2003: Wissenschaftliche Buchgesellschaft.; Mircea Eliade, Ioan Couliano: *Handbuch der Religionen*, German Zürich 1991: Artemis & Winkler.
10 Of the University-teaching books in Germany only Margrit Pernau: *Transnationale Geschichte*, Göttingen: Vandenhoeck & Ruprecht, 2011 has an own chapter: p. 117–131. As one might have expected, here area-studies are history of India. The two other "Lehrbücher" Andrea Komlosy: *Globalgeschichte. Methoden und Theorien*, Wien: Boehlau 2011 (hereafter Komlosy *Globalgeschichte)* and Sebastian Conrad: *Globalgeschichte. Eine Einführung*. München: Beck, 2013 treat religious questions in other contexts. An up to date introduction is Gerald Faschingeder: Religionen. Die Wiedergeburt des Religiösen im globalen Austausch, in: Reinhard Sieder, Ernst

The essay is written in English, first of all, because as a lecture it was offered at the 39th Conference of the Political Economy of the World System in Berlin March 2015.[11] This essay is part of a corpus of texts stemming from that conference.[12] Secondly the essay is written in English, since that is the global language of our time.[13] Two centuries ago it might have been written in Latin. In regard to some habits criticised as "Anglobalism"[14] my point is simple: this essay neither is presupposing, that English historiography is leading in this field, nor, that German is; it is just offering a critique of the latter one with a special emphasis on World-System-Studies.

Langthaler Hg.: *Globalgeschichte 1800–2010*, Wien: Boehlau 2010, p. 503–528.

11 Hans-Heinrich Nolte: Bericht zur 39. Tagung der Gruppe POLITICAL ECONOMY OF THE WORLD SYSTEM Berlin 2015: http://geschichte-transnational.clio-online.net/tagungsberichte/id=5937

12 Publication of the other contributions is in progress in three volumes, edited by Manuela Boatcă, Andrea Komlosy and Hans-Heinrich Nolte:
   1. Global inequalities with paradigm-publishers, New York;
   2. Worldregions, Migrations and Identities as volume 14 of the series "Zur Kritik der Geschichtsschreibung", published with Musterschmidt, Gleichen
   3. Coloniality of Power and Hegemonic Shifts as issue of the Journal for World-System Research.

13 I am grateful to William Clarence-Smith, Andrea Komlosy and Manuela Boatcă for critique. Of course, mistakes are mine.

14 „Anglobalism" here means a habit to consider as first rate what has been published in English without prior comparison to historiography in other languages. Of course this critical term comes from Latin-America: Elpidio Laguna Diaz: Kulturbegriff und Geschichtsschreibung. Gegen eine Anglobalisierung, in *Zeitschrift für Weltgeschichte*, (hereafter *ZWG*) 7.2 (2006) p. 43–52.

There is no attempt to cover all or at least some of the historiographies to the question – neither English, nor Russian, Chinese, Italian etc., etc.. An essay on the role of religion in global historiography would have to establish at least three or four "national" examples and then start with comparisons.[15] In case this essay does invite comparisons, that would be very welcome. Of course – since English is the global language, in my argument English texts play a big role, and I am content, that the New Cambridge World History regularly offers chapters on religion as also the Companion to World History edited by Doug Northrup.[16]

For an English-language public it might be adequate to give a note to my person: I am a German born 1938 in Ulm, migrated around in my country and had the luck to be invited for a year in High-School in the US. I studied history and German studies in Marburg, Münster and Göttingen and became professor for History of Eastern Europe in Hannover.[17] History of Eastern Europe is my "Area-Studies", and my research mostly was on Russia respectively the Soviet Union. Since four from ten of the case-studies presented

---

15 As Dominic Sachsenmaier: New Perspectives on Global History, Cambridge 2011: Cambridge UP has done for a different subject.
16 Doug Northrup Ed.: *A Companion to World History*, Oxford 2012: Blackwell.
17 I did my Dr. phil. with Reinhard Wittram, see his *Das Interesse an der Geschichte* Göttingen 1954: Vandenhoeck & Ruprecht and cf. below; and Alfred Heuss, see his *Zur Theorie der Weltgeschichte* Berlin 1968: Walter de Gruyter. My professor in German studies was Albrecht Schöne, see now his *Der Briefschreiber Goethe*, München 2015: Beck.

below are from this field, let me give some introductory notes to the field.[18]

From my friends and colleagues in Hannover I learned about the ubiquity of Nazi-crimes in my country, about Africa and about "glocalism".[19] Colleagues from many European countries took part in a row of conferences on internal

---

[18] For terms see Sergei Pushkarev: *Dictionary of Russian Historical Terms*, New Haven 1970: Yale University Press; Hans-Joachim Torke Hg.: *Lexikon der Geschichte Russlands*, München 1985: Beck; Glossary in *Quellenbuch*. Basic Manfred Hellmann, Gottfried Schramm, Klaus Zernack, Stefan Plaggenborg Hg.: *Handbuch der Geschichte Russlands,* Vol. 1–5, Stuttgart 1981–2003: Hiersemann (hereafter *Handbuch*). For a fine overview see Christoph Schmidt: *Russische Geschichte 1547–1917*, München 2009: Oldenbourg. For a post-Soviet Russian narrative see Institut Rossijskoj Istorii RAN Ed.; A. N. Sakharov Main Redactor.: *Istorija Rossija* Vol. 1–3, Moskva 1996: AST. My own attempts cf. note 1.

[19] Marlis Buchholz u. a. Hg.: *Nationalsozialismus und Region*, Festschrift Herbert Obenaus, Bielefeld 1996: Verlag für Regionalgeschichte; Helmut Bley: Das 20. Jahrhundert aus der Sicht eines Afrikahistorikers, in *ZWG* 10.1 (2009) S. 9–29; Christiane Schröder, Heike Düselder, Detlef Schmiechen-Ackermann u. a. Hg: *Geschichte, um zu verstehen*. Festschrift Carl-Hans Hauptmeyer zum 65 Geburtstag, Bielefeld 2013: Verlag für Regionalgeschichte; Florian Grumblies, Anton Weise Hg.: *Unterdrückung und Emanzipation in der Weltgeschichte. Zum Ringen um Freiheit, Kaffee und Deutungshoheit*, Hannover 2014: Jmb-Verlag. The new generation of historians in Hannover has turned to Atlantic Studies, see Ulrike Schmieder, Hans-Heinrich Nolte Hg.: *Atlantik*, Wien 2010: Promedia = Edition Weltregionen Vol. 20 (hereafter Schmieder *Atlantik*).

peripheries, which I organised.[20] Most of my colleagues and friends in Russian studies, who took part in discussions in many conferences between Moscow and St. Petersburg, Lipetsk and Volgograd, contributed to a volume on historiography of both dictatorships, which are entangled in our history. The volume also was published in Russian.[21] With many of my colleagues and friends in Vienna I had the luck to cooperate in the projects "Globalgeschichte"[22] and/or "Weltregionen".[23] With my friends and colleagues in the "Verein für Geschichte des Weltsystems" I learned about global history of traffic, migrations, slavesystems, global inequality, empires and nation-building, hegemonic shifts and coloniality of power, about India, Central-Asia, China and the Americas.[24] Last but not least with and from Christiane Nolte I learned about Bal, Bel or Belum from Mesopotamia and the trinities of Egypt.

---

20 Cited more extensively in Hans-Heinrich Nolte: Zentrum und Peripherie in Europa aus historischer Perspektive, in: *Aus Politik und Zeitgeschichte*, Beilage zu Das Parlament, 63.6 (4. Februar 2013) S. 36–41; Online: www.eurotopics.net/fluter.de/ hanisauland.de/apuz/izb/deutschlandarchiv.
21 Hans-Heinrich Nolte Hg.: *Auseinandersetzungen mit den Diktaturen. Russische und deutsche Erfahrungen*, Gleichen 2005: Musterschmidt = Zur Kritik der Geschichtsschreibung 9; Russian M. B. Korchagina Ed.: *Izuchenie diktatur. Opyt Rossii i Germanii*, Moskva 2007: Pamjatniki istoricheskoj mysli = Rossijskaja Akademija Nauk, Serija Rossija+Germanija+Evropa vypusk 6.
22 Peter Feldbauer, Bernd Hausberger, Jean-Paul Lehners Hg.: *Globalgeschichte. Die Welt 1000–2000*, Vol. 1–8, Wien 2008–2012, Wien: Mandelbaum (hereafter Feldbauer *Globalgeschichte*).
23 Andrea Komlosy Geschäftsführende Hg.: Edition Weltregionen, Bd. 1–23., Wien 2000–2015: Promedia.
24 See www.vgws.org, and chronologically the „Rundbriefe" there. The reviews in the *ZWG* are edited by Manuela Boatcă.

Mostly during retirement I have published some attempts on World-History, although I do not read any Asian language.

For my mistakes in writing English I ask for kind indulgence. Since English is the global language of today, I think the dons will have to accept a lot of local colours to keep its creativity. Let me cite John Agard (who coming from Guyana of course had a more difficult Journey to London market than someone coming from Ulm on the Danube, and the Caribbean coast I am taking on here is still more strange to me than the English one of the language):[25]

> "me not no Oxford don
> me a simple immigrant
> from Clapham Common
> I didn't graduate
> I immigrate ..."

I.2 World and Global History – on concepts

Following the classical differentiation I use „World-History" for an encompassing view of what happened in the past of mankind, while I use "global history" for worldwide interconnections between its different parts, countries or settlements.[26] Within Global history I think the concept of a World-System, which Immanuel Wallerstein proposed and

---

[25] Cited from Jana Gohrisch: Transatlantischer Kulturaustausch, in Schmieder *Atlantik* p. 209–225, here p. 222. On the ups and downs of global languages see Nicholas Ostler: *Empires of the Word*, New York 2005: Harpers; and more systematically Harald Haarmann: *Weltgeschichte der Sprachen*, München 2006: Beck.

[26] Bruce Mazlish: Die neue Globalgeschichte, German in: *ZWG* 3.1 (2002) p. 9–22.

elaborated,[27] has the merit of structuring the development of European economy and of the accumulation of powers on the European continent in space and time[28], from the period of the expansion of Christian powers in the late Middle Ages (see below) to that of European global pre-eminence under British hegemony between 1815 and 1941 and the period of American hegemony 1941–1991. Between 1450 and 1991 this part of Global history may well be discussed in the terms of Centre (USA, Europe, later Japan) Semi-Periphery (Russia, Spain, Argentina) and Periphery (colonies, "Third World"). For explaining the period following the breakdown of monopoly-socialism and the rise of China and India the concept does not seem to fit very well. Wallerstein is arguing, that the system has come to its end and a "bifurcation" of trends opens up new possibilities,[29] while others argue, that the US has turned into an Empire,[30] and still others think, that the system might be reorganised, maybe under US-hegemony but

---

27 Immanuel Wallerstein: *The Modern World-System*, Vol. 1–4, New York – Berkeley, Academic Press – California UP 1974–2011; German Vol. 1–4, Frankfurt – Wien 1986–2012: Syndikat – Promedia.

28 Immanuel Wallerstein: The Inventions of TimeSpace Realities, in The same: *Unthinking Social Science*, Cambridge Polity Press 1991, p. 135–148; German in The same: *Die Sozialwissenschaften "Kaputtdenken"*, Weinheim: Beltz-Athenäum 1995, p. 164–180.

29 Immanuel Wallerstein: *Utopistics*, New York: The New Press, 1998; German Wien: Promedia, 2002.

30 Helmut Prantner: Imperium USA. Die aktuelle englischsprachige Argumentation, in ZWG 14.2 (2013) p. 135–158; Hans-Heinrich Nolte: Die USA – Imperium oder globale Nation? In Ders. Hg.: *Imperien*, Schwalbach 2008: Wochenschau; Herfried Münkler: *Imperien. Die Logik der Weltherrschaft* München 2005: Beck.

with strong competitive members as China or India.[31] History of religions might be of help in these discussions, not only, because religions as noted above are important today, but also, because some religions have much longer histories than the European World-System or other systems. Systems of course have histories, they are started and ended, as for instance the system of khanates in the steppes of Central-Asia from the breakup of the Mongol Empire to the partition of Mongolia between Russia and China (1309–1689).[32]

My research in World-System-Studies,[33] started 1980 with the argument, that in order to define the limits and structure of the System you have to do research in social, political and religious history just as much as in the history of economy, which was the focus of Wallersteins first book. It followed, that following more political and religious criteria the history of Europe as a system started in the fight between religious and secular universal institutions in the 12th and 13th centuries.[34] Here, following Immanuel

---

[31] This was debated in the cited congress, see note 11, and Salvatore Babones: The Once and Future Hegemon, in *The National Interest* 138 (July/August 2015) p. 54–62.

[32] Bert Fragner, Andreas Kappeler, Hg.: *Zentralasien. 13. bis 20. Jahrhundert. Geschichte und Gesellschaft.* Wien: Promedia, 2006; Nolte *Weltgeschichte 1*, p. 38–43.

[33] Hans-Heinrich Nolte: – Zur Stellung Osteuropas im internationalen System der Frühen Neuzeit. Außenhandel und Sozialgeschichte bei der Bestimmung der Regionen, in *Jahrbücher für Geschichte Osteuropas (hereafter JbGOE)* 28 (1980) p. 161–197. English *in Review VI/1 (1982)* p. 25–84.

[34] For a comparison of differing chronologies see Komlosy: *Globalgeschichte*. p. 188–210.

Wallersteins "Unthinking",[35] I propose some unthinking for the World-System-Analysis.

Regarding methods all such questions start with interdisciplinarity. My first research more than half a century ago in Göttingen was guided by the Lutheran historian Reinhard Wittram, a "Baltic German" who had been "resettled" from Latvia in 1939 and had sided with National-Socialism up to 1945.[36] My research was situated between the disciplines theology and history.[37] Following 1968 first Marxist and second Weberian sociology took the part of theology. To put my thinking on interdisciplinary research into a nutshell – I think, that historians need sociologists for constructing historical narratives, and that sociologists, just as theologians, need historians for learning about the hard facts.[38]

My work on religions, following 1968 changes in my work as historian, took Marx' note as starting point, that the political and historical importance of religion will last as long, as the world is organised in a way nobody can

---

35 Wallerstein: *Unthinking*; cf. Immanuel Wallerstein: Der Weg der Weltsystem-Studien oder wie man vermeidet eine Theorie zu werden, ZWG 2,2 (2001) p. 9–32.

36 Cf. Błażej Białkowski: *Utopie einer besseren Tyrannis. Deutsche Historiker an der Reichsuniversität Posen (1941–1945)* Paderborn: Schöningh, 2011.

37 Hans-Heinrich Nolte: *Religiöse Toleranz in Rußland 1600–1725*, Göttingen: Musterschmidt, 1969; The same: Verständnis und Bedeutung der religiösen Toleranz in Rußland, in *JbGOE* 17 (1969) S. 494–530.

38 Immanuel Wallerstein u. a.: *Die Sozialwissenschaften öffnen. Ein Bericht der Gulbenkian Kommission zur Neustrukturierung der Sozialwissenschaften*, German Frankfurt/Main: Campus, 1996.

understand.[39] I added Ernst Blochs reasoning, that religions show an *"Überschuss"*, – an intellectual excess over what the rules of society are.[40] The belief in equality before God (for instance) shows the hope of men for more solidarity, however unequal the reality may be. Already Walter Benjamin, then a contemporary to Bloch, in his review pointed to the messianic character of the secular aim of an individual "right to happiness" (as the American declaration of independence put it).[41] This intellectual point of departure was appropriate for the topic religion in Soviet society which I researched in the 70ies and 80ies,[42] but it was not sufficient.

---

39 Karl Marx: *Das Kapital* Vol. 1, Hg. Institut für Marxismus-Leninismus beim ZK der SED. Berlin; Dietz, 1966 = MEW 23, p. 94. „*Der religiöse Widerschein der wirklichen Welt kann überhaupt nur verschwinden, sobald die Verhältnisse des praktischen Werktagslebens den Menschen tagtäglich durchsichtig vernünftige Beziehungen zueinander und zur Natur darstellen*"...

40 Ernst Bloch: *Atheismus im Christentum. Zur Religion des Exodus und des Reichs* [1968] New edition Frankfurt: Suhrkamp, 1973, p. 262 „*Denken lässt sich nichts vormachen [...] Statt der Historie und statt der Rückstände aus schlechter Entzauberung zeigt dann die Emanzipation selber ihre christologischen, ihre messianischen Züge. Dergleichen liegt weit über dem bloßen Erbe, etwa an den gewaltigen Kulturwerken, deren Gewalt wie Tiefe mit religiöser Ideologie und deren Überschuß verbunden sind....*"

41 Walter Benjamin: Theologisch-politisches Fragment, in Ders.: *Sprache und Geschichte*, Edition Stuttgart 1992: Reclam = Reclam 8775, p. 132 f., here p. 132: „*Die Ordnung des Profanen hat sich aufzurichten an der Idee des Glücks*".

42 Hans-Heinrich Nolte: Budgetakkumulation, Kollektivierungskampagne und Religionsbedrückung im ersten sowjetischen Fünfjahrplan, in *Kirche im Osten* 24 (1981) p. 83–105; The

The obvious way to enlarge the intellectual apparatus was reading Max Weber.[43] I used Cologne-testimonies mostly from the 17th century for discussing the thesis of Protestantism and Capitalism.[44]

The concept I am working with now, almost two academic generations and a couple of paradigm-changes later, I call recurring on Shmuel Eisenstadt[45] and Willfried Spohn "comparative-civilizational multiple modernities perspective"[46] with a special focus on systems – on actions of powerful people in Churches and states, of social players, traders and representatives of transnational groups within relations between a couple of political entities (states).[47] Following the

---

same: Religiosität und Unterschichten in der sowjetischen Gesellschaft in *Gegenwartskunde* 1981/2 p. 177–186; The same: Die Glaubensgemeinschaften und die Religionspolitik des Staates, in Gottfried Schramm Hg.: *Handbuch der Geschichte Rußlands* Bd. 3,2 (1856–1945), Stuttgart: Hiersemann 1992 p. 1709–1741

43 Max Weber: *Wirtschaft und Gesellschaft. Grundriss der verstehenden Soziologie* (1920), Hg. Alexander Uhlig, Frankfurt: Zweitausendundeins 2006.

44 Hans-Heinrich Nolte: Kapitalmentalität und Rentenmentalität. Ein rheinisch-niederländisches Beispiel zum Thema Protestantismus und Katholizismus, in *Das Argument* Sonderband 103, Berlin: Argument-Verlag 1983, p. 20–30.

45 Shmuel N. Eisenstadt: Vielfältige Modernen, German in: *ZWG* 2,1 (2001) S. 9– 34.

46 Wilfried Spohn: Power, in: Said Amir Arjomand Ed.: *Social Theory and Regional Studies in the Global Age*, Albany NY: New York UP, 2014 (hereafter Arjomand *Theory)*, p. 113–143, here p. 121.

47 I do not see systems as acting by themselves, see lately Harald Kleinschmidt: Repräsentanten des großen Ganzen. Bemerkungen zu Systemmodellen … in *ZWG* 16.1 (2015) p. 95–134.

13th century we may speak of the European World-System. Economic, political and last but not least religious actors from the center of the system dominated and structured the "rest" of the world in the long 19th and short 20th centuries. We do not know yet, whether the actors from USA and EU will try to go on with this hegemony, or whether we are on the verge of a century, where the actors will accept a new role – acting as representatives of two "global provinces" – to adopt Chakrabartys famous formula.

I.3 Religions and civilizations

During the "cultural turn" research on religions has gained momentum in the contexts of "civilizations." Huntingtons book,[48] which has given new impetus to this discussion,[49] to a considerable degree is taking concepts from Oswald Spengler,[50] who again might be seen as the most pessimistic – and in view of the 2nd World War last – voice in a pan-European debate of the 19th and early 20th centuries. The debate was started by Heinrich Rückert[51], and carried on by Sir Charles Dilke[52]

---

48 Samuel P. Huntington: *Der Kampf der Kulturen* [1996] German 5th ed. Wien: Europaverlag 1997.
49 Hans-Heinrich Nolte: Zur Reichweite von Kulturkreiskonzepten, in Peter Nitschke Hg.: *Der Prozess der Zivilisationen: 20 Jahre nach Huntington*, Berlin: Frank & Timme, 2014.; p. 65–86.
50 Oswald Spengler: *Der Untergang des Abendlandes. Umrisse einer Morphologie des Abendlandes* [1918] Hg. Von H. Werner, München: Beck, 1963.
51 Heinrich Rückert: *Lehrbuch der Weltgeschichte in organischer Darstellung*, Leipzig: T.O. Weigel, 1857.
52 Charles Wentworth Dilke: *Greater Britain – a record of travel in English-speaking countries*, 4th ed. London: Macmillan, 1869.

and Nikolaj Danilevskij.⁵³ Religions played a big role in this debate, Spenglers millenarianism and his idea of apocalypse even became a topos of everyday-life.⁵⁴ The four cited concepts of culture are biologistic, they assume that human organisations function like plants – they start as seeds, grow, bear fruit and die. Of these four the concepts of the British politician Dilke MP and of the German professor Rückert were racist. In the concepts of the two others, of the Russian biologist Danilevskij and the German writer Spengler, cultures are defined by a combination of languages, habits, institutions and traditions of thinking, but also are seen as plants: they grow and decay.

Quite often these "cultures" are characterized de facto mainly by religions. The borders Huntington is drawing are defined by religious adherences.⁵⁵ For instance his border between East- and West-Europe is following an approximate line between Protestantism and Catholicism including the Union of Brest on the one and Orthodoxy on the other side (but not taking into account the historical differences between Belorussia and Galicia regarding the Union).⁵⁶ Ferguson's contemporary apocalypse of the West though is recurring more on generational decay of institutions, habits etc. and is secular.⁵⁷

---

53 Nikolaj Jakovlevich Danilevski: *Russland und Europa* [Russian 1888]; German [1920] Osnabrück: Otto Zeller, 1965
54 Dina Gusejnova: Der Prophet als Parfum. Das Spenglersche am europäischen und amerikanischen Modernismus, in *ZWG* 15.1 (2014) S. 141–162.
55 Huntington op. cit. p. 30 f.
56 Huntington op. cit. p. 235.
57 Niall Ferguson: *Der Niedergang des Westens. Wie Institutionen verfallen und Ökonomien sterben* [2012] German Berlin: List, 2014.

Also in the definitions of cultures not so rarely religious facts are used as characteristics without evaluating the contexts. For example, in the West it is quite common to interpret the Russian or even the Soviet State as "Third Rome". It is true, that Christians (not only Orthodox ones) believed for a long time in the interpretation of the dream of Daniel,[58] that the fourth Empire is the Roman one, which will last till the last day. In the Orthodox churches Constantinople was considered as the "new Rome". When it was conquered in 1453, some Russian clerics argued, that now Moscow should be seen as the third, the last, one.[59] The concept was popular in the 16th century, but already then created a confrontation with the Greek clergy, who retained the title "new Rome" for Constantinople.[60] The Russian power-elites liked to listen to this thesis about their role in history, but did not accept it as binding theory. Up to the "eternal peace" between Moscow and Poland 1686 the Russian elites were careful not to come into an open conflict with the Ottoman Empire and even returned the fortress of Azov to it, which Cossacks had taken in 1637.[61]

---

58 Daniel chapter 7.
59 For a convincing study see Hildegard Schaeder: *Moskau. Das Dritte Rom* [1929] 2nd Edition Darmstadt: Wissenschaftliche Buchgesellschaft, 1957; A. V. Kartashev: *Ocherki po istorii Russkoj Cerkvi*, Moskva; Terra, 1993, Tom 2, p. 121–124.
60 *Quellenbuch* Nr. 2.12: foundation of the Patriarchy Moscow.
61 From the view of orthodoxy N. F. Kapterev: *Kharakter otnoshenij Rossii k prvoslavnomu vostoku*, ²Sergiev Posad: M.S. Eov, 1914 p. 349–382. cf. Michael Khodarkovsky: *Russia's Steppe Frontier*, Bloomington/ Indiana: Indiana UP (University Press, hereafter UP) 2002, here p. 131. See also *Quellenbuch* Nr. 2.40.

By the way – there had been a *"Renovatio Imperii Romanorum"* (renewal of the Roman Empire) in the West in 800, which lasted up to 1806. To characterize Russian-Orthodox culture by a theological position held by clerics for more than a century, while disregarding more than a millenium of real existence of the "Holy Roman Empire", does seem to be a case of double standards. The question, why Rome had fallen and the Lord had not returned yet, was one of all Christianity, and legitimized the surprising (and completely self-deceptive) concept, that Rome did not fall at all ....

Since histories of religion as a rule are better established as academic disciplines than histories of cultures, the paradigm "cultures" often has a touch of evasiveness – what may be well researched in the field of Church-History might be presented as new because the paradigm claims novelty. This argument also is concerning research following the paradigm of "social-economic" history, not only in the question of confessions and social discipline sketched below, but also in reconstructing the status of persons. My example is from early-modern Muscovy: the difference between *kholopy* and *jasyry* (Orthodox serfs and Muslim slaves) was first of all in religion, from which social and economic differences followed.[62]

Histories of religions, at least those of religions "with a book", quite often started scientific discussions and set standards, which contributed to changes in the societies in which they prospered. The critic of "Constantines Donation" in the 15th century (Nikolaus von Kues, Lorenzo Valla) questioned the legitimacy of the power of the Catholic Church "in the

---

62 Hans-Heinrich Nolte: Jasyry: Non-Orthodox Slaves in Pre-Petrine Russia, in publishing in Christoph Witzenrath Ed.: *Eurasian Slavery, Ransom and Abolition in World History 1500–1860*, Farnham: Ashgate, 2015.

world";[63] the critic delivered by the *"Leben Jesu Forschung"* in the 19th century (David Friedrich Strauss) put an end in believing the bible word for word in the academic world; and the debate on Davids und Salomons Kingdom (Israel Finkelstein and Neil Asher Silbermann) in the 21st century in the academic world put an end to what we learned about the kingdom of Israel in bible-school.[64]

Cultural similarities and dissimilarities between religions and religious milieus as parts of world-history may not adequately be researched without the expertise of religious history. We should neither presuppose, that a certain region is characterised by a "culture" nor exclude this possibility, and always keep in mind, that most religions address humanity and not only the population of a region or a nation. For the relations between nations and religions see below, but also regions only rarely are settled just by followers of one religion. There may be specifics – for instance it is my thesis, that Eastern Europe up to 1917 was more characterised by religious tolerance, than Western Europe was.[65] That does contribute to the explanation of history in that period, when

---

63 Birgit Emich: [Papsttum] Kirchenstaat in Friedrich Jaeger Hg.: *Enzyklopädie der Neuzeit* [Translations to English being published online with Brill, Leyden] (hereafter EdN) Vol. 1–16, Stuttgart: Metzler, 2005–2012. Of course – since the papal state continued till 1870 – also it showed, how limited the effects of such critic may be.

64 Israel Finkelstein, Neil Asher Silbermann: *Keine Posaunen vor Jericho*, German München: Beck 2001; Israel Finkelstein: *Das vergessene Königreich. Israel und die verborgenen Ursprünge der Bibel*, German München: Beck 2014.

65 Hans-Heinrich Nolte: Osteuropäische religiöse Kulturen, in *EdN* 9.

ethno-religious groups carried on in the East, whose counterparts in the West had been assimilated or expulsed long ago. But then religious history is not the whole story – economy, politics (like the ascent and decline of Empires),[66] social developments, the traffic-revolution, ideology are "subsystems" also. Research should therefore start with a more formalistic and more geographic concept like "World-Regions",[67] and from there may go to World-History.

---

[66] Examples in Jane Burbank, Frederick Cooper Eds.: *Empires in World History*, Princeton: Princeton UP, 2010; Herfried Münkler Ed.: Was Imperien leisten = ZWG 11.2 (2010); Michael Gehler, Robert Rollinger Hg.: *Imperien und Reiche in der Weltgeschichte*, 2 Vols. Wiesbaden: Harrassowitz 2014.
[67] Komlosy: *Globalgeschichte* op. cit. p. 166–188; without the term „world-regions" Pernau: *Transnationale Geschichte*, p. 95–116.

II Case-Studies

II.1 Some famous ones

On the role of religions in World History I shall neither present the most famous cases as religion in India, which inter alia Said Arjomand and Sujata Patel have sketched,[68] nor elaborate on the problems of Islam and Secularism.[69] Also I only recall, that the oldest world-systems are religious ones, which started two and a half millennia ago in the "Achsenzeit".[70]

We are accustomed to writing global history of religions in the sense of worldwide connections and entanglements, especially in the histories of expansions, what in Christianity would be called history of missions. But it was and is more than that – transnational and transcontinental intellectual exchange by preaching and by books[71] and by travelling persons, by "preachers".[72] Examples are many: for instance the Buddhist monk, who founded the Wild-Goose-Pagoda in

---

68 Said Amir Arjomand: Three generations of Comparative Sociologies, and Sujata Patel: Gazing Backward or Looking Forward, in Arjomand *Social Theory* p. 1–23, and p. 437–460.
69 Asli Vatansever, Christian Lekon Hg.: Islam und Säkularisierung = *ZWG* 16.1 (2015).
70 Karl Jaspers: *Vom Ursprung und Ziel der Geschichte* [1949], Frankfurt: Fischer, 1959, Axial Age p. 11–80; cf. Johann P. Arnason: Historicising Axial Civilizations, in Arjomand *Social Theory* p. 179–202.
71 Michael Mitterauer: *Warum Europa? Mittelalterliche Grundlagen eines Sonderwegs*, München: Beck 2003, p. 235–271.
72 Nayan Chanda: *Bound together. How Traders, Preachers, Adventurers and Warriors Shaped Globalization*, New Haven/Conn.: 2007, Yale UP

Xi'an in China in the 7th century, Ibn Battuta from Tanger, who lived as a Muslim teacher and even *Kadi* in many countries between Mali and China in the 14th,[73] and the Herrnhut missions, which connected the small German village of that name governed by the Count of Zinzendorf to the Caribbean, to South Africa and to India in the 18th and 19th centuries.[74]

II.2 Catholic Church and European World System in the 13th century

The history of the Catholic Church is well researched.[75] The wealth of the Churches constituted between one Fourth and one Third of the public wealth up to early modern times, and was rendered part of modern fiscal means by secularisations[76] – changed into fiscal or princely property. Not so rarely ecclesiastical wealth was changed into merchant or industrial capital directly. It is argued for a region like Constance, where Church-property was not transferred into capital, that this was one of the reasons for falling back economically in the 19th century[77].

---

73 Tim Mackintosh-Smith Ed.: *The Travels of Ibn Battuta* (1958) new edition London: Picador, 2003.
74 Jan Hüsgen: Zwischen Anpassung und Widerstand. Nationalhelfer in der Mission der Brüdergemeine; Claus Füllberg-Stolberg: Christliche Mission und Doppelemanzipation von indigener Bevölkerung und Sklaven in Südafrika, in *ZWG* 15.1 (2014) p. 65–116.
75 Introductory Peter Walter: Römisch-Katholische Kirche in *EdN* 11; cf. Nolte: *Weltgeschichte* 1. p. 113–140.
76 Hans-Heinrich Nolte: Säkularisationen und Säkularisierungen, in *ZWG* 16.1 (20115) p. 11–34.
77 Gert Zang: A Region on its way to the Periphery, in: Hans-Heinrich Nolte Ed.: *Internal Peripheries in European History*, Göttingen: Musterschmidt, 1991 p. 153–168.

To my judgement[78] the history of Europe as a system started in a fight between religious and secular institutions in the 12th and 13th centuries – in a period of internal theological strifes and external expansions[79]. It had a prehistory in the early middle ages in the kingdoms of the Burgundians, Visigoths, Francs or Langobardians, with independent churches as Spanish and Irish playing a role some time. But small kingdoms and small churches had a poor stand against the attempts of Pope and Emperor to re-establish the Roman Empire in the centuries following Charlemagne. Philip T. Hoffmann takes the divisions of the Carolingian Empire following the death of Charles I. as start of the failing of Empire,[80] but thinking in families, not offices was part of all society in that period and did not preclude the continuation of the Empire. The project "Renovation of the Roman Empire" was successful for a few centuries and failed only in the consequence of the fight between the Emperor and the Pope about religious matters in 12th century.[81]

Otto 1st had founded his Renovation of the Empire 963 on cooperation between the king of Germany and its bishops. The king and Emperor, relying on his royal status as cleric and his influence in designating the higher church-officials, used the Church as his bureaucracy and in return donated much land to her. But the radical reformists on the side of

---

78 For a comparison of concepts see Komlosy: *Globalgeschichte* p. 188–210.
79 Luis Suarez Fernandez: Église et hérésies en Occident; Jean Richard: L'expansion européenne: les croisades, in: Hélène Ahrweiler, Maurice Aymard Eds.: *Les Européens*, Paris: Hermann 2000, p. 145–164.
80 Philip T. Hoffmann: *Why did Europe conquer the World?* Princeton 2015: Princeton UP
81 Cf. ibidem p. 132–134.

the Church attacked this construction and accused the king and Emperor of simony, of buying Church-offices. The Emperor lost, and when Frederic II. von Hohenstaufen reopened the fight based on the inherited potential of the kingdom of "both Sicilies", he lost again. In the end his grandson, the German king Konradin, was beheaded on the marketplace of Naples 1268, ordered by Charles, now king of Sicily and brother of king Louis IX. of France.

Not the Pope won the battle though, on the contrary: in 1309 the pope went to Avignon. The winner was the house of Anjou.[82] France was the kingdom with most inhabitants and most probably most potential in Christendom; but the Anjou did not want to follow the obviously unhealthy German path of renovation of the Roman Empire. Latin Christianity turned into the European World System – European not only, because in its first centuries it was limited to this continent, but also, because there have been other systems in World-History. The European World-System included independent kingdoms, aristocratic republics and the Holy Roman Empire as a member, which though generally was less powerful than France or Spain. All these states were competing with one another. But the system was kept together by the Church, the monastic orders, the universities with the use of the same teaching language from Oxford to Paris and Prague to Bologna, and of course by trade. The Church stayed highest judge in all theological questions and in all cases relating to sex and marriage.

The Church also was a "secular" power in many states stretching from the Rome to Cologne and Salzburg to Riga, from the order of Calatrava in Castile to the order of the German knights on the shores of the Baltic Sea. From the very

---

[82] Dieter Berg: *Die Anjou-Plantagenets*, Stuttgart: Kohlhammer, 2003.

beginning the European World System had a centre – not a single town or a single country, but the "Banana" of industrious and wealthy regions from Florence to London. The system had a semiperiphery – from western Poland to northern Spain – and peripheries, oversea-colonies from the Baltic to Greece and the Crimea, and overland-colonies from Spain south of the Duero-river to Poland east of the Bug-river.[83]

"Central Institutions as papacy and empire ... lost importance in the face of the pluralistic development of the pluralistic European statesystem", as Alfred Kohler summarizes in his history of the 16th century,[84] but it was a long fight. The Church was powerful and rich, and ideas of an universalist Empire were alive. Church and Habsburg yet another time combined their means to have Charles V. elected in the face of French opposition and growing Protestant protests in Germany, but soon the politics of the Emperor, directed at a "universal monarchy", turned the Pope into an enemy. The *conquista* of the Americas did not change the configuration of powers in Europe. Spain was able to win Italy, but despite the victory at Pavia in 1525 was not able to turn Germany into a more centralised, more effective state under Habsburg leadership. Rather Saxony strengthened it's autonomy in the context of the religious issue (despite military defeat) and called for the intervention of France. The development went in the direction of the peace of Westphalia 1648 – Habsburg remained the most important power in the centre of Europe, but many of

---

83 Hans-Heinrich Nolte: The European System in the Middle Ages. Pleading for a set of indicators and nonlinear research, in M.Hroch, L. Klusakova Hg. *Criteria and Indicators of Backwardness, Essays on Uneven Development in European History*, Praha 1996: Faculty of Arts, Charles University Prague, 1996, p. 29–46.
84 Alfred Kohler: *Neue Welterfahrungen. Eine Geschichte des 16. Jahrhunderts*, Münster: Aschendorff 2014 p. 167.

the electorates and dukedoms of Germany developed in the direction of sovereign states. But in all these states "the connections between Church and worldly powers were close."[85]

We may summarize, that the role of the Church for the nascent European World System was central – on the one hand in helping to defeat all attempts to recreate an Empire, and on the other hand in keeping Catholic Christianity together by religious rules and habits – Latin as common language, universities organised by religious orders, considerable wealth of the Church especially in landed estates, organising the cooperation of Christian powers in crusades and arbitrations, and of course in keeping morals.

II.3 Protestantism and nation-states in the 16th cy. "Konfessionsbildung" and social discipline

For the princes and kings the wealth of the Church was a lure; from Henry VIII.[86] to Gustav Wasa the Reformation[87] spelled increase of means by secularisation of Church-properties. But the Reformation also brought more control and more capacity to influence, to form the population. And by translating the bible into popular languages the reformation furthered a new movement: national self-consciousness.

The defeat of Roman universalism in the 13th century might have been interpreted as a late justification of the

---

85 Kohler *Welterfahrungen* p. 205.
86 Data Christopher Hill: *Von der Reformation zur Industriellen Revolution. Sozial- und Wirtschaftsgeschichte Englands 1530–1780*, German Frankfurt: Campus 1977 p. 25
87 Introduction S. Ehrenpreis, U. Lotz-Heumann: *Reformation und konfessionelles Zeitalter*, Darmstadt 2002 (WBG); Nolte *Weltgeschichte* 1 p. 113–140; Hans-Heinrich Nolte: Religions et confessions, in Ahrweiler *Europénnes*. p. 279–286.

Orthodox Church, in which the Patriarch in Constantinople was a Primus inter pares, the bible was translated into different languages and new Patriarchies were founded – if some prince had enough power and means.[88] But at the very beginning of the 13th century Christian knights mainly from France and Christian traders mainly from Venice had destroyed the East-Roman Empire in the 4th crusade.

In late medieval times in Western Christianity (which for three centuries consisted only of Catholic kings and noble republics) some groups called themselves nations, for instance the nobility of Poland. They kept their ethnical allegiances, even in case they started to use Polish *"po pansku"* – as the nobility talks. A formula was: „*gente Ruthenus, natione Polonus*" sum – which may perhaps for the 21st century be translated as: "I am an Ukrainian and belong to the noble brotherhood, which is governing Poland".[89] Also students used the word nation. In the university of Prague all students coming from the North of Bohemia constituted the Saxon, all from the West the Bavarian and all from the East the Polish nation. At that time a student – "*scholarius*" – was an ecclesiastical person, who had taken the lower vows and following these was unmarried. The nations lived together and cared for one another; for instance at the university of Paris Germans, Dutch, English and others from the North lived and

---

88 Vlassios Phidas: Église orthodoxe d'Orient, in Ahrweiler *Européenes* p. 135–144.
89 Manfred Alexander: *Kleine Geschichte Polens*, Stuttgart: Reclam, 2003, p. 100; Joerg K. Hoensch: *Geschichte Polens*, ³Stuttgart 1998 (ulmer), p. 111 f.

made student politics together in the "English nation". Of course this was not, what we understand as nation today.[90]

I follow Liah Greenfield in her judgement, that the first modern political nation developed in England. Participation of the English elites in parliament already was established in the 13th century, but the inclusion of nobility, gentry and towns into the political nation was a phenomenon of Tudor-England.[91]

Religion played a central part in this construction of the English nation. To quote Trevelyan: "In the course of Elizabeth's long reign, the younger generation, brought up on Bible and Prayer Book, and sharing the struggle for national existence against Spain, Pope and Jesuits, became for the most part fervent Protestants. Bible reading and family prayer were becoming customs of the English."[92] The biblical story, published in many sermons, was that of the morally sound and healthy small nation Israel against the whore Babylon – the virgin against sinful Empires suppressing freedom and with sexually deviating courts – not only young women for Louis XIV., but even young men for Catherine II. Sadly enough for the British this topos migrated along with the Puritans to the new world and was turned against London in the 18th century. The colonists, representing their thirteen states and not yet one state, used the image of small nations fighting against a tyrant and

---

90 For the history of this and related terms see Reinhard Koselleck and others: Volk, Nation, Nationalismus, Masse in: *GG* 7, p. 141–431.
91 Liah Greenfield: *Nationalism*. Cambridge/Mass: Harvard UP, 1992.
92 G. M. Trevelyan: *English Social History* (1944) 9th edition Cambridge: Longmans, 1948, p. 180 f.

Great Britain; "with a firm reliance on the protection of Divine Providence".[93]

The new nations were characterized by republicanism. The medieval movement of the estates claiming and implementing political participation was transferred into modern capitalist codecision, common rule of the rich and the king. There were different forms – the seven States of the Netherlands partly were governed by peasants, partly by merchants and partly by nobility – united by the reformed Church; in England two houses had been developed – one for the "Lords" of Church and Nobility, one for the "commons" formed by wealthy agrarian businessmen and merchants of the towns, united by the Anglican Church.[94] In both nations some of the excluded groups were constituted by religion – Catholicism and differing protestants.[95]

Institutionalising in England started in the 13th century but was stabilised in 1688 by the "Glorious Revolution" and the Bill of rights. The two republican nations of the 17th century were more stable in their politics and more effective in raising taxes and in borrowing, and that way they were

---

93 The unanimous Declaration of the thirteen united States of America (sic), July 4, 1776, in: David Saville Muzzey: *A History of our Country*, Boston/Mass. 1953 (Ginn) p. i–iii.

94 Hans-Heinrich Nolte: Radikalisierung von Macht und Gegenmacht, in Margarete Grandner, Andrea Komlosy Hg.: *Vom Weltgeist beseelt, Globalgeschichte 1700–1815*, Wien: Promedia, 2004 p. 45–72.

95 J.S.A.M. van Koningsbrugge: The >Generaliteitslanden< as a Periphery of the Republic, in Nolte *Internal Peripheries* p. 119–132; Hans-Heinrich Nolte: Zwischen Duldung und Vertreibung. (Ethno-)religiöse Minderheiten im Vergleich, in: Sylvia Hahn, Andrea Komlosy, Ilse Reiter Hg.: *Ausweisung, Abschiebung, Vertreibung in Europa*, Innsbruck 2006 (Studien-Verlag) p. 26–47.

more successful than the Empires and absolutist kingdoms.[96] The condition for the success of parliamentarism was what Max Weber has coined "*Abkömmlichkeit*"[97] – those (limited) groups, who have the right to vote, must command enough wealth to take their time for doing politics.

The Protestant reformation in the beginning, take the year 1521, was a fundamentalist religious movement, bent on defining the rules of religion and life „*sola scriptura*", alone by the bible. This fundamentalist radicalism adequately was used for legitimating the Great Peasant War in Germany 1525. The Emperor Charles V. was determined to crush the Protestant heresy, but he never found the time to really do it. Rather it turned out to be the job of the Protestant princes to fence the fundamentalists in, which indeed they did.[98]

Following the reformation in Saxony the prince – one of the seven electors of the king of Germany (the future Emperor) – became highest bishop, if only in external matters, not in questions of theological truth (*summepiscopus in rebus externis*). In 1526–30 the elector ordered "visitations" of the parishes, starting a control-system of the pastors and the parishioners, which ensured, that all parishioners visited divine services, listened to the sermons, which also were used as information system of the government ("*Kanzelabkündigungen*"), behaved "like Christians" and sent their children to bible-school. They learned to live following artificial time and to work with emphasis, labour being considered as part

---

96 Nolte *Weltgeschichte 1* p. 286–308; Peer Vries: *State, Economy and the Great Divergence* London 2015: Bloomsbury.
97 Weber *Wirtschaft und Gesellschaft* p. 1052–1054.
98 Wolfgang Reinhard: Sozialdisziplinierung – Konfessionalisierung Modernisierung, in: Nada Boškovska Leimgruber Hg.: *Die Frühe Neuzeit in der Geschichtswissenschaft*, Paderborn 1997: Schöningh, p. 39–56; Nolte *Weltgeschichte 1,* p. 261–267.

of Christian living. This *"wertrationale Arbeitswilligkeit"* (willingness to work following values)[99] definitely helped Saxony become the industrial centre of Middle Germany.

In most Calvinist communities this institutionalising of a new social discipline was not enacted via a state-church but via the congregations – legend has it, that curtains were not welcome in Dutch villages and towns, in order to grant the elder brethren an easy look onto their younger brethren's family-life. Any drinking? Any fancy dresses? Any playing of cards, "the devils playthings"? Were the members of the community really at work? Catholics nota bene followed up in many regards after the Council of Trent.

"Confessionalizing"[100] meant much more than belonging to a certain confession – it meant learning a new social discipline, part of the "change in structures of affects and controls" Norbert Elias wrote about."[101] Discipline at work, no drinking, no fussing around ... That is not to say, that religion was the only way to enforce this new social discipline. But the new social discipline, whether enforced by a German "Landeskirche", the High-Church of England and Scottish congregations was part of (multiple) transitions to new roles in the World System.

The transitions from Empires to nation-states within the WS went along up to the 21st century. Both Empires and nations were, in France up to the revolution but in many

---

99 Weber: *Wirtschaft und Gesellschaft* p. 113. For a new history of labour see Andrea Komlosy: *Arbeit*, Wien 2014: Promedia.
100 I find an up to date translation in the title of a CFP: „Konfessionen als verhaltensprägender Faktor" (Religious Denominations as a Factor of Behavior): https://hsozkult.geschichte.hu-berlin.de/termine(id=26881 (consulted May 11th 2015).
101 Norbert Elias: *Über den Prozeß der Zivilisation* (1936) Neuausgabe Frankfurt: suhrkamp 1976 here p. ix of Elias new introduction 1968. Cf. Gleichmann: *Soziologie*, p. 231–306.

countries till today, structured along alliances of "Throne and Altar". That meant, that when Empires (using the term here in the popular sense of the 19th century) were broken up, old ecclesiastical differences (as Catholicism in Ireland or the Union of Brest in the Ukraine) or dissenters (like the new Hussite Church in Czechoslovakia) gained new importance. You need good reasons for breaking up a state, and for Mazaryk these included seeing democracy, in contrast to monarchy, as religiously legitimated.[102] For the US it is "in God we trust", as the $ tells every user everyday. These national limitations of Christianity, which actually is universalistic in character, always contained some elements of selfdeception, but that did not impair their effects.

Without religion it neither is possible to understand Spinoza's *"deus sive natura"* (God or nature) nor Leibniz's "prestabilized harmony". Religion was an input in the intellectual debates from Early Modern times to the present. The input started with the wording of enlightenment: from Jesus as light – "Life was in him, and his life was the light of all mankind"[103] – to the light of pure reason (and back from there to the longing for the night of the early romantics). Religious topoi and concepts were secularized and used as parts of the new modern languages, as Albrecht Schöne has shown for German literature more than half a century ago.[104]

---

102 Hans-Heinrich Nolte: Die demokratische Nation als Mythos. Überlegungen zum Werk Th.G.Masaryks, in Adelheid von Saldern Hg.: *Mythen in Geschichte und Geschichtsschreibung aus deutscher und polnischer Sicht*, Münster: LIT, 1996, S. 172–182
103 Johannes 1, 4. Compare also Matthew 5.14 ff. inter alia.
104 Albrecht Schöne: *Säkularisation als sprachbildende Kraft*, Göttingen: Vandenhoeck & Ruprecht, 1958.

II.4 "Old belief" as protest against the modernising tendency of the Russian Orthodox Church in the 17th century

In the middle of the 17th century the Russian Orthodox Church[105] started a reform of its holy texts by comparing them to the Greek originals.[106] This theological *"ad fontes"* – to the sources – was parallel to the Renaissance-movements for the correct texts of the bible of Erasmus or Hutten, while two centuries later, and it was Orthodox, meaning it was looking for the East-Roman tradition (which we are used to call Byzantine). The reform led to important changes of the divine service, it was supported by the hierarchy and many of the studied clergy (mostly "black", who had taken monk vows), but most of the white clergy, married ministers who carried the brunt of the parish-work, opposed it bitterly. The hierarchy argued, that in the years following the conquer of Constantinople by the Ottomans mistakes had encroached in the holy books in Russia, while the opponents argued, that the Greek books could not be correct, since Greeks lived in a country governed by Muslims and paid money for their toleration.

In 1666 a Church-council of the Russian Orthodox Church was summoned with guests from all over the Orthodox world from Constantinople to Aleppo and Alexandria. It took place in Moscow and confirmed the reforms, but the opposition did not yield. From now on they were persecuted

---

105 A. V. Kartashev: *Ocherki po istorii Russkoj Cerkvi*, 2 Bde. Moskva: Terra 1993; Thomas Bremer: *Kreuz und Kreml*, Freiburg: Herder 2007.

106 Serge A. Zenkovskij: *Russkoe staroobrjadchestvo*, München: Fink 1970; new ed. Moskva *DI-DIK*, 2006; Nickolas Lupinin: *Religious Revolt in the XVIIth Cy.*, Princeton/NJ.; Kingston Press, 1984.

as *raskolniki* – schismatics, people who split the Church; also they were called oldbelievers or oldritualists.

In classical cooperation between Church and State following, in the East as in the West, the letter of the bible, that there will be one shepherd and one flock,[107] the Russian elites attempted to eradicate the schism by force.[108] They put leading oldbelieving teachers as Protopriest Avvakum to the stakes and simply forbade old rituals. But the believers saw in the reforms a religious and cultural change of enormous importance; in fact many believed, that the end of the world had come.[109] They interpreted the year of the Church-council 1666 as the number, which characterizes the beast in the Apocalypse[110] and reckoned, that since the Tsar had changed sides, Moscow – and for them it was the Third Rome – had fallen. In this view Daniel's dream also seemed to prove, that secular Empires were crumbling and Christ was coming a second time. The oldbelievers fled the government, some crossed the borders – towards the Ottoman Empire, towards Poland and Sweden, and maybe even to the Americas.[111] Many went to the woods and started living in monastic communities waiting for the Lord. When government-troops came to force them back into the common flock, they rather choose to "flee to the fire" – to burn themselves. Communities of ten or twenty,

---

107 Johannes 10, 16.
108 For the history of the persecution see Nolte *Religiöse Toleranz* op. Cit. p. 122–176.
109 *Quellenbuch* Nr. 2.42.
110 Apocalypse 13,18.
111 My interpretation of the fact, that Spanish ships found Russian settlements in 48° north on the Pacific coast of America in 1789: Hans-Heinrich Nolte Hg.: *Geschichte der USA I*, Schwalbach 2006: Wochenschau = Studien zur Weltgeschichte, here p. 109 f.

but in some cases of more than a thousand people committed collective suicide.[112]

When the young Tsar Peter 1st in his attempt to modernize Russian weapons-industry in Carelia in 1702 came close to such a community (in Vyg[113]) the oldbelievers were ready for collective suicide again, but the Tsar agreed to keep a distance, as long as those living in that monastery would work in the ironworks of Olonetsk, producing weapons for the war against Sweden. Later the Tsar hoped to end the schism by forcing all oldbelievers to pay double taxes. In order to enforce that, the Synod (see below) ordered the eparchies to keep lists of all parishioners who gave confession once a year. Those who did not were to be questioned (if "need be", questioned painfully) whether they were true believers or not.

The Tsar was trying to introduce religious politics coming from the West into Russia, but the bureaucratic structure to enforce them was missing. Russia did not have a bureaucracy capable of controlling the people continuously. Double taxes for common Russian people were almost impossible to bear.[114] Every oldbeliever tried to evade them, meaning in the countryside, that every person put on the list would flee. But then his village would have to pay his part of the taxes, since in Russia at that time the villages were liable for the amount of taxes once established for the whole village. That meant, that no villager would ever betray the oldbelieving neighbour to the "*Syshchik*" or commissary, who came to keep the list,

---

112 Hans-Heinrich Nolte: Selbstvernichtung religiöser Gemeinden in der Geschichte, in *Journal für Geschichte* 1979, S. 20 f.

113 Robert O. Crummey: *The Old Believers and the World of Antichrist*, Madison: Wisconsin University Press 1970.

114 For an overview of the taxes see Richard Hellie: *The Economy and Material Culture of Russia 1600–1725*, Chicago: Chicago UP, 1999, p. 536–570.

rather the villagers (mostly supported by the owner of the estate) would beat the commissary up. It proved impossible to implement Peters program.[115]

But where "*Sozialdisziplinierung*" – establishing the new discipline – in early modern times failed, as in Russia in Peters time, it did not exist, leaving the training of the new habitus – for instance living following artificial and not natural time – to later periods.

To sum up: Religion in Early Modern Times in Russia offered an intellectual possibility for opposition against modernising politics of the government. It was defeated – but Russia failed to implement the social discipline, which in most Protestant and some Catholic parts of Europe was going along with "*Konfessionalisierung*" – confessionalizing Christianity (which, *mutatis mutandis*, also happened in Islam and Buddhism[116]).

II.5 The Russian Orthodox Church serving enlightened absolutism in the 18th century and yet loosing the Patriarchy and monasteries

With considerable costs Russia in 1589 had established the Patriarchy Moscow, the fifth Patriarchy in the Orthodox World.[117] Less than two centuries later Peter 1st ended it and introduced a "*Collegium*" as head of the Church.[118] In imitating competition he followed the example of his main enemy

---

115 Hans-Heinrich Nolte: Die Reaktion auf die spätpetrinische Altgläubigenbedrückung, in *Kirche im Osten* 19 (1976) p. 11–28.
116 Nolte *Weltgeschichte 1*, p. 268–270.
117 *Quellenbuch* Nr. 2.12.
118 Igor Smolitsch: *Geschichte der Russischen Kirche 1700–1917* Leiden 1964: Brill.

Sweden. In the beginning he even wanted to call this college of bishops *"Konsistorium"*, but then was persuaded to use the old Orthodox name of Synod for it.[119] Why did he decapitate the Russian Church?

The Church had been the strongest estate in the *Sobor,* the "assembly," where Church-hierarchy, high nobility and great merchants of Russia met for discussing politics.[120] His half-sister and competitor for the Throne Sofija still had convoked it, but Peter did not do so during in his reign, and by abstaining ended this institution of participation and established absolutism in Russia.[121] While it ever would be risky to have a possible "second head" to the Empire – there were some clergymen who looked to Catholic examples, for instance Patriarch Nikon during the reign of Peters Father –, Peter could hope, that some members of the Synod would be on the side of enlightened absolutism, for instance Feofan Prokopovich, bishop from Pskov.[122] First of all the Tsar called for religious support for his program of militarisation, but second he asked for an end (or at least reduction) of contemplative life and for more active work – he limited the monasteries and ordered them to provide for the veterans of his armies. The Russian Church had put more weight on contemplation

---

119 N. F. Kapterev: *Patriarch Nikon i tsar Aleksej Mikhajlovich*, 2 vols. Sergiev Posad: M. S. Elov, 1909–1912 .
120 L. V. Cherepnin: *Zemskie sobory Russkogo gosudarstva v XVI–XVII vv.*, Moskva: Nauka, 1978; Hans-Joachim Torke: *Die staatsbedingte Gesellschaft im Moskauer Reich*, Leiden: Brill, 1974.
121 A. N. Medyshevskij: *Utverzhdenie absoljutizma* v *Rossii*, Moskva: Tekst, 1994.
122 Viktor Smirnov: *Feofan Prokopovich*, Moskva: Soratnik, 1994. His defence of absolutism was translated to German, excerpt *Quellenbuch* 3.15.

and less on social works as both Western Churches. Peter wanted to break this intellectual – or, as the clergy would put it – philosophical tradition.

As noted above, Churches played a decisive role in establishing schooling in Early Modern Times, not only in Saxony. The Russian Orthodox Church in the 18th century had no tradition in parish-schools (except schools for the clergy), differing from both the Lutheran Church of Sweden and the Catholic Church of Poland in this regard. Peter I. tried to found a secular schoolsystem, but he was not able to implement it as a countrywide institution, just as later Catherine II. failed in a similar attempt. Only in the 19th century the Russian Orthodox Church started establishing schools in every parish.[123] The importance of religion for history here was, that up to that date the Russian Church did not supply the society with a service, which western Churches offered since the 16th or 17th century.

Last but not least the Emperor Peter I. had a look at the wealth of the monasteries. Already Tsar Aleksej had tried to increase control and income of the State by establishing a *monastyrskij prikaz*, an office for the monasteries and ran into the opposition of the hierarchy. In Peters time the Synod kept control, but the Church donated heavily on all patriotic occasions (as for instance the building of the different Navies of the Empire). "Only" in 1762 the Emperor Peter 3rd, also Duke of Lutheran Holstein, dared to implement secularization of the properties of the monasteries.[124]

---

123 Jens Bruning: Schule in: *EdN* 11, here also Hans-Heinrich Nolte: [Schule in] Osteuropa .Cf. *Quellenbuch* 2.71, 2.72.
124 *Quellenbuch* Nr. 3.19.

II.6 Islam as an anti-colonial movement in the Caucasus in the 19th century

An immediate political and economic context of religion[125] was and is Muslim fundamentalism as a way to fight the predominance of enlightenment as propagated by the Western centre. Russia may be an especially interesting example, since enlightened expansion of Christianity here was organised by an autocratic empire, while France in Algier or Britain in the North-Western-Province of India both claimed parliamentary constitutions for their home-countries. Some parallels between the wars of the Northern Caucasus, conquered by the Russian Empire only in 1858, British expansion into the North-Western territory, where Lord Durrand in 1893 drew the line to divide the Pashtun-People as it seemed fit for the defence of India, and French conquering of Algier in 1830 seem obvious.[126] Chechens living in Moscow, Pashtun in London und Algeriens living in the banlieus of Paris have their place in the long trajectory of Christian expansions in the 19th century. All three places today are hotbeds of terrorism.

The Russian Empire was multinational and multi-religious, and within that frame there was a long history of Islam.[127] In

---

125 Generally Andreas Kappeler: *Russland als Vielvölkerreich*, München: Beck 1992 ; Hans-Heinrich Nolte: Osteuropäische religiöse Kulturen, in: *EdN* 9, Stuttgart 2009.
126 For a fine comparison of Russian Caucsasus und French Algiers see Vladimir Bobrovnikov; Russkij Kavkaz I Francuzskij Alzhier, in: Martin Aust, Rikarda Vulpius, Aleksej Miller Hg.: *Imperium inter pares*, Moskva: Novoe literaturnoe obozrenie 2010, p. 182–203.
127 Dictionary Alexandre Bennigsen, S. Enders Wimbush: *Muslims of the Soviet Empire*, London: Hurst 1985. P. G. Landa: *Islam v istorii Rossii*, Moskva 1995

the Russian Empire, differing from Latin Europe, Muslims – like members of most other religions – were tolerated,[128] although Orthodox missions (which did not have much success) were supported by the Tsar[129] and for a career in state-services Muslims had to accept baptism. When in the 19th century Russia expanded as one "member of the family" of imperialist states,[130] the number of Muslim subjects multiplied. Many Muslim states or groups put up fights when incorporated, just as the people of the Northern Caucasus.

Although already in the 16th century Cossacks had conquered some territory on the Terek-River in the North-Caucasus, only in the 2nd half of the 18th century Russia actively intervened on the side of Orthodox Georgia and then annexed that same kingdom in 1801.[131] In a war against Persia Russia conquered Baku and Aserbaijdzhan north of the Araxes (or Aras-River) in 1803.

Only the region east of the Transcaucasian road from Vladikavkaz/Groznyj to Tiflis/Tbilisi, south of the Terek-River, west of the coast of the Caspian Sea till Derbent and north of the Mountain-range remained independent. This mountainous country of about the size of Switzerland was and is inhabited by some 30 different ethnic groups. Most of these speak Caucasian or Turk languages and are Sunni-Muslims; only the Ossetians to the West speak an Indo-Germanic language close to Armenian and confess Orthodoxy, while

---

128 Nolte *Toleranz* p. 54–89.
129 Hans-Heinrich Nolte: Umsiedlungen als Instrument der Mission im Wolgaraum 1740–48, in *JbGOE* 45 (1997/ 2) p. 199–209.
130 Susan P. Mccaffray, Michael Melancon Eds.: *Russia in the European context 1789–1914. A Member of the Family*, New York 2005: palgrave.
131 Roin Metreveli: *Georgia*, Nashville/Tennessee: Publishers International, 1995, p. 75–83.

part of the Lesghiens in the East speak a Caucasian language and confess Judaism; the latter are called "Mountain-Jews". Most Caucasian ethnic groups used transhumant grazing for their cattle and were in danger of losing their winter-pastures in the steppe to Cossacks and Russian confederates (as Buddhist Calmuks and Muslim Nogaj Tatars) with the advance of the Empire.

Many thought, that it would not take much time for the Russian Empire to include this territory, the nobility of which already had tendencies towards the Empire. But under the leadership of the Nakhsbandija-brotherhood and Sufi-influence Sheikh al-Gazi-Muhammad-al-Awari ad Dagistani united the country and his students "led the people to religion and *Sharia*" as the Dagestani-scholar Nadir ad Durgalis put in (the 1930ies).[132] Gazi in 1832 "called for obedience to the Sharia, for living according to its rules, and for rejection of the *Adat*" (local rules) ... "and he collected troops for visiting towns and villages in order to lead the sinful back to the right path, to strengthen the weak and destroy the criminal nobility in the villages.." The nobility fled to the Russians, the wine "found in the basements of their houses" was poured out.[133] The Russians intervened and Gazi fell in battle. He third Sheikh leading the defence was Shamil.[134]

In 1844 Shamil routed a Russian army, which had followed his troops into the mountains. He organised the Muslim State in regions, led by *kadis* (Muslim law-scholars and judges), not by clan-chiefs or nobility. He had a couple of

---

132 Michael Kemper, Amri R. Sixsaidov Hg.: *Die Islamgelehrten Daghestans*, Berlin: Klaus Schwarz, 2004, p. 106 f...
133 A. M. Barabanov Hg.: *Chronika Muchamedda Tachira Al-Karachi*, Russian Moskva/Leningrad: Nauka, 1941, S. 41.
134 Cf. *Quellenbuch* Nr. 3.57–3.59; M. M. Bliev, V. V. Degoev: *Kavkazskaja Vojna*, Moskva: Roset, 1994.

factories for powder and rifles built and a cannon-foundry organised by an engineer, who had studied in a *Medresa* in Kairo. The Russians for some time did not dare to attack him again. They held the coast along the Caspian Sea, but lost many men when attacking through the valleys running up to the highlands and the crest of the Mountainridge. The Russians built defensive lines all around this Muslim territory, and Shamil was not able to take advantage of the Crimean war. In 1858 a Russian campaign crossing the mountainridges into the highlands defeated the Sheikh. He ended his life in exile in Kaluga in Southern Russia.[135]

His memory is living on, in the wars of the Chechens for a sovereign Muslim national state (and not only autonomy) from Moscow, but also in those terrorist groups fighting for a *Sharia* based Muslim emirate embracing all North-Caucasus with its many nations (in which then the Christian Ossetians and the Mountain-Jews would be religious minorities). The Nakshbandija-brotherhood survived Soviet times and formed the basis of the new Muslim movements in Post-Soviet-Times.

II.7 Christian Democracy as European variant for politics in the 20th century

Writing History with secular France and pragmatic Britain in focus may be misleading for the history of Middle and Eastern-Middle Europe. Germany and Italy, Austria and

---

[135] For the older literature see Moshe Gammer: *Muslim resistance to the tsar: Shamil and the conquest of Chechenia and Daghestan*, London 1994: Frank Cass.

Czechoslovakia did develop into stable nations of the centre only by the development of Christian-democratic Parties.[136]

When the Peace of Vienna brought considerable Catholic German territories under the rule of Protestant states, Catholics started thinking about political possibilities within the growing democratic movements. The Papacy in the doctrine of infallibility in *ex cathedra decisions* just had shown, that it stuck to absolutism, but anyway some Catholics started to think more favourably about democracy. In Germany Ludwig Windthorst[137] took part in starting a democratic Catholic party – the "Zentrum" –, which, following the defeat of Austria and Hannover in 1866, developed into the second oppositional party within the new Reich.[138] This Catholic Party had a political program of social compromise without ever advocating revolution as the Social Democrats did at that time. In 1918 the "Zentrum" became one of the founding fathers of the Weimar republic, but in 1933 it voted for Hitlers "Ermächtigungsgesetz".

Following 1945 the newly founded "Christian Democratic Party", combining Catholic and Protestant political groups, became the political main stay of post-war Germany. Konrad Adenauer, who before 1933 had been "Lord Mayor" of Cologne and had survived Nazism in the service of Catholic institutions, grew into its figurehead. The CDU

---

136 Michael Gehler, Wolfram Kaiser, Helmut Wohnout Hg.: *Christdemokratie in Europa*, Wien: Boehlau, 2001.
137 Hans-Georg Aschoff: *Rechtsstaatlichkeit und Emanzipation*, Sögel: Emsländische Landschaft, 1988; Rudolf Morsey: *Wegbereiter der Christlichen Demokratie*, Köln: Katholische Sozialwissenschaftliche Zentralstelle 1991.
138 Günther Rüther Hg.: *Geschichte der Christlich-Demokratischen und Christlich-Sozialen Bewegung in Deutschland*, Vol. 1–2, Bonn: Bundeszentrale für politische Bildung, 1984.

fathered what became known as "Rhineland capitalism", which by state-intervention avoided some of the sharper forms of social differentiation in income and living standards as in "Manchester capitalism" without ever calling the fundamentals of capitalism in question. The role of Christian Democracywas fending off trends to the left and implementing considerations for social balance and, in a mild form of green politics, for the creation – see Angela Merkels exit from atom-power. In Italy the "Democracia Christiana" played a similar role, also in Austria the "Österreichische Volkspartei".[139] The Christian-Democratic Parties also belonged to the founding movements of the European Union. It would be misleading to write the history of the European Union mainly as history of states signing conventions; in fact Catholic and Protestant networks had considerable influence in the process of Union.[140]

During the last half of the 20th century Germany and Austria were politically stable and economically quite successful. Therefore they have been seen as models for development by political groups in other nations of the center or the semiperiphery of the European system.[141] One example is Turkey – there though

---

[139] Michael Gehler, Wolfram Kaiser, Helmut Wohnout Hg.: *Christdemokratie in Europa im 20. Jahrhundert*, Wien: Boehlau, 2001.

[140] Wolfram Kaiser: Christdemokratische Netzwerke und die Genese Kerneuropas, in: Michael Gehler, Wolfram Kaiser, Brigitte Leucht Hg.: *Netzwerke im europäischen Mehrebenensystem*, Wien: Boehlau, 2009 p. 87–104.

[141] Jürgen Elvert, Jürgen Nilson-Sikora Hg.: *Leitbild Europa?* Stuttgart: Steiner 2009.

with a differing, own political agenda, based upon Islam and making front against a secular military-based State-party.[142]

II.8 Secularisation as European "Sonderweg"

In the old "Universal History" religion occupied an important place since Herder, and even in the secularized forms of Hegels "*Geist der Völker*" respectively "*Weltgeist*". Today quite often European intellectuals expect, that religions will loose importance continuously; maybe not connected with a revolution, for which Marx had predicted the "*Verschwinden*" (vanishing) of religion, but as a trend. Following WWII there was a renaissance of religion in World-History, but the late fifties and the coming of consumer-society in Europe did seem to prove the point.[143] The impression indeed was and is, that we are living in "a secular age".[144] But at the end of the century it became clear, that only the European societies had secularised – in quite different forms, by the way[145] – while

---

142 Asli Vatansever: Die Muslimbrüder und die AKP, in *ZWG* 14.2 (2013) p. 159–182; the same: Säkularisierung trotz Laizismus, *in ZWG* 16.1 (2015) p. 51–62.
143 Herrmann Zabel: Säkularisation, Säkularisierung, in; Otto Brunner, Werner Conze, Reinhart Koselleck Hg.: *Geschichtliche Grundbegriffe*, (herafter GG) Bd. 5, Stuttgart 1984 (Klett-Cotta) S. 789–829; Friedrich Wilhelm Graf: Säkularisierung,: Ulrich Hufeld: Säkularisation, Friedrich Wilhelm Graf: Säkularisierung in EdN 11; Hans Joas, Klaus Wiegandt Eds.: *Säkularisierung und die Weltreligionen*, Frankfurt: Fischer, 2007.
144 Charles Taylor: A secular Age [2007], German: *Ein säkulares Zeitalter*, Frankfurt: Suhrkamp, 2012.
145 Hans-Heinrich Nolte: Säkularisationen und Säkularisierungen, in Asli Vatansever. Christian Lekon Eds.: *Islam und Säkularisierung* = ZWG 16.1 (2015) S. 11–34. In that text I propose a difference in wording between secularization for turning

in "the rest of the world" including the Americas[146] religious affiliation had changed to considerable degrees, but societies outside of Europe had not become secular.[147]

This might be the point to turn to the question, whether the "Bezbozhnye", the Union of Atheists in the 1920ies and 1930ies was not a fundamentalist movement also. They fought all religions of the Soviet-Union, from Islam to Orthodoxy and from the Rabbis of the different Jewish groups (between the Crimea, the Caucasus, Buchara and Kiev) to the Lutheran, Mennonite or Catholic pastors of the German "colonists." Sometimes they fought with fundamentalist fervor, smashing icons, turning churches into stables, taking reliques from the altars and throwing them on the ground to show, that the bones were rotten.[148] Maybe that would be another topic. But strangely enough the atheist pressure from the Communist Party also created religious communities – oldbelievers escaping once more to the woods and starting separate villages, Orthodox in expectation of Christ's Second Coming (it really was easy to see, who was the red dragon mentioned in

---

    Church-property over to laymen,(which has been considered necessary by believing people since millenia) and secularizing for diminishing or abolishing religious influence in "the world" (which implies less rigorous or no belief) .

146 Hartmut Lehmann: *Säkularisierung. Der europäische Sonderweg in Sachen Religion*, ²Göttingen: Wallstein, 2007.
147 Ulrich Willems, Detlef Pollack, Helene Basu and others Eds.: *Moderne und Religion. Kontroversen um Modernität und Säkularisierung*, Bielefeld: transcript-Verlag, 2013.
148 For first arguments see N. P. Krasnikov Hg.: *Po ėtapam razvitija ateizma v SSSR*, Leningrad 1967: Nauka; or S. D. Skazkin Hg.: *Nastol'naja kniga ateista*, 8th edition Moskva 1985: Izdatel'stvo politicheskoj literatury.

the Apocalypse[149] this time) or new Baptist groups who held divine services lasting many hours in private rooms.[150]

In this context we should also raise the question, whether the German genocide against the Jews really followed secular delineations. One has to keep in mind, that the secular, racist argument was thought up completely, it was an invention. "Race" as such is a pseudoscientific concept for the analysis of humans[151], but on top of that to define blond and blue-eyed Jews of the neighbourhood as belonging to a different "race", (singling out those, who looked more Mediterranean), simply was ideological deception and self-deception in order to offer a seemingly scientific, secular ideology. We might follow the interpretation, that this deception just was invented to exclude and mark those who were to be grabbed and exiled[152] (and following 1941 to be murdered systematically). But that shortcut would be insufficient. There was no obvious biological difference like skin-colour in Germany, and the Nazis knew that. While pretending to be scientific in reality German anti-semitism followed religious lines: Everybody, who did not belong to the Mosaic creed, had to prove that by looking for his "Arian" grandparents. Since sim-

---

149 Apocalypse 12.3.
150 See my Religiosität und Unterschichten in der sowjetischen Gesellschaft in *Gegenwartskunde* 1981/2 S. 177–186; Bremer: *Kreuz*, bes. S. 136–142.
151 Werner Conze: Rasse in GG 5, p. 135–178.
152 This robbing of a religious minority was officially supported by German state-institutions as in the following case the Oberfinanzdirektion Hannover: Claus Fuellberg-Stolberg: „Wie mir bekannt geworden ist, beabsichtigen Sie auszuwandern" … in: Carl-Hans Hauptmeyer, Beate Eschment, Udo Obal Hg.: *Die Welt querdenken*, Frankfurt: Lang, 2003, p. 219–234.

ply it was not possible to divide the Germans by biological markers all people had to write their *"Stammbaum"* (their genealogical tree), and in order to do that they had to ask the pastors, whether their grandparents had been baptized or not.[153] Also in the genocide in Eastern Europe[154] – in those cases, where living in a *Shtetl* and talking Yiddish did not mark the victims sufficiently[155] – the murderers looked for circumcision; which means they looked for the effect of a religious ritual (because of that some, if very few, Jewish soldiers of the Soviet Army taken prisoners of war survived pretending to be Muslims).[156]

Secularization rather looks like another European *"Sonderweg"*. This has consequences in praxis, not only within the NS-regime, but also today. If for instance young Europeans meet young Afghanis, Africans or Indians in villages and every-day life, the secular Europeans cannot answer the

---

153 The first anti-Jewish laws (*Nürnberger Gesetze*) assumed, that it was clearcut, who was a Jew, but then many disputes made an official definition necessary. A biological definition was impossible, therefore in the Verordnung zum Reichsbürgergesetz (14.XI.1935) a religious one was given:*„ § 2. Jüdischer Mischling ist, wer von einem oder zwei der Rasse nach volljüdischen Großelternteilen abstammt [...] Als volljüdisch gilt ein Großelternteil ohne weiteres, wenn er der jüdischen Religionsgemeinschaft angehört hat."*

154 Il'ja Al'tman: *Opfer des Hasses. Der Holocaust in der UdSSR 1941–1945* [Moskva 2004], Gleichen: Musterschmidt 2008 = Zur Kritik der Geschichtsschreibung 11.

155 As example: Ljuba Abramowitsch, Hans-Heinrich Nolte: *Die Leere in Slonim*, Dortmund: IBB, 2005.

156 Pavel Poljan: *Obrechennye pogibnut'. Sud'ba voennoplennykh-evreev vo Vtoroj Mirovoj Vojne*, Moskva Novoe izdatel'stvo 2006, p. 44–51.

questions of their believing friends, what they are – Muslims? Christians? Jews?[157] Rupert Neudeck, a member of the Catholic left in the Rhineland and friend of Heinrich Boell and Franz Alt, recently has recalled, that secularizing of everyday life in his home-region happened only in the sixties and seventies, meaning within his lifetime.[158] It happened and it changed the cultures of Europe, but up to now it did not change the religious cultures of "the rest".

The discussions about fundamentalism[159] and about "Secularizing and the Return of Religion"[160] are offering further reasons for an attempt to reevaluate the role of religions in world-history. When German or British young men go to Syria to fight in the ranks of Sunni-Muslim fundamentalists against a Shia-based government and some more secular, but certainly also Muslim reformists, the need for at least contemporary histories of religions does seem to be obvious.

II.9 The role of religions in the developing East-West-conflict in Europe

We are witnessing a new East-West-conflict within Europe. It is developed on the one side by Catholic Poland in

---

157 Lecture of the founder of the NGO "Cap Anamour" for saving illegal migrants on the high Seas Rupert Neudeck in Barsinghausen/ Germany April 28th 2015.
158 Rupert Neudeck: *Radikal leben*, Gütersloh: Gütersloher Verlagshaus, 214, p. 98–108.
159 Clemens Six, Martin Riesebrodt, Siegfried Haas Hg.: *Religiöser Fundamentalismus. Vom Kolonialismus zur Globalisierung*, Innsbruck 2004: Studienverlag.
160 Albrecht Koschorke: >Säkularisierung< und >Wiederkehr der Religion< in Willems. *Moderne* p. 217–260.

cooperation with Germany lead by the Christian Democratic Union, and on the other side in close cooperation between the Russian leadership and the Russian Orthodox Church. In fact Patriarch Kirill has legitimised a call for unity "Of course the Russian Orthodox Church, the Church of the intellectually indivisible Russia, may not divide the united people of God following political, national, social or any other principle."[161] If we read that statement in the context of Church-History, it means, that the Patriarchat should not be divided, that there should not be new obedience's – while not only the question of Union, but also the question of an autonomous (αυτοκεφαλος) Ukrainian Church is one of the points of the agenda. President Putin even took the fact, that Prince Vladimir conquered Cherson to force the Emperor in Constantinopel to give a πορφγρογένεθη, a daughter of Emperors for marriage in return to accepting baptism, as argument for a Russian character of the Crimea.[162]

In Germany the argument is appearing as completely secular: Russia by annexing the Crimea has violated international law[163] and its own commitment in the Budapest Memorandum 1994.[164] Both arguments are true, and definitely the break of international commitments should not go unreprimanded. But there does seem to be a religious fervour behind the German insistence on lawfulness. In deed international law does not accept a onesided declaration of independence;

---

161 *Quellenbuch* 7.55.
162 *Quellenbuch* 7.54, compare the excerpt from Nestors Chronicle *Quellenbuch* 1.4.
163 The „Deutsche Gesellschaft für Osteuropakunde", leaving aside calls for neutrality of a scientific society in politics, has supported that point: *Quellenbuch* 7.56.
164 *Quellenbuch* 7.49.

before becoming effective, the other side has to consent.[165] When Germany wanted to implement the sovereignty of the Kosovo against Serbia though, it did not wait till Serbia accepted that loss of this region, but recognized its independence immediately. Therefore there might have been reasons to take the breakaway of the Crimea from the Ukraine with more self-criticism and offer Russia ways out of its mistake.

But whether or not religious, if secularised commitments or the Catholic Church itself played a role in German politics regarding the Ukraine, the religious background obviously is important. As noted above the fight between the "Latin" and the "Greek" parts of Christianity go back to medieval times. The "Byzantine" renovation of the Roman Empire led to the conquering of Italy. There it was seen as "Greek", and these Greeks controlled much of southern Italy for centuries and transferred the obedience of the bishoprics to Constantinople. Bari, the last stronghold, was taken by the Sicilian Normans only 1071 – and these returned the obedience of Southern Italy to Rome. An aggressive image of Byzantine was developed, for instance in the novel of King Rother – you could not trust them, they are not fighting openly, and they do not give their beautiful daughter to the knight coming from the West, so that he has to use tricks. Is that the image of an enemy with less power? 1204 Constantinople was taken in the 4th crusade, and the *"ecclesia triumphans"* – the Catholic Church in its triumph – enforced the Primate of Rome – mostly by western colonies on Greek soil, which on the long run were not able to defend against the Ottoman Empire.

Following the Lithuanian/Polish expansion to the east in late medieval times obedience's were changed in

---

165 Jörg Fisch: *Das Selbstbestimmungsrecht der Völker. Die Domestizierung einer Illusion*, München 2010: Beck.

East-Middle-Europe. 1589 the Russian Church became Patriarchate, which intensified the question, where the many Orthodox people in the eastern territories of Poland/Lithuania would belong. 1596 most Orthodox bishops of Poland joined the Union of Brest and accepted the *Primate* of Rome, but most believers decided against the Union, militarily relying on the Cossacks. In 1653 Russia was involved into the fight and in 1686 the Ukraine was divided between Russia and Poland along the Dnepr.[166]

In the divisions of Poland 1772–1815 most territories with members of the Union came to Russia, and the Tsar forbade it (not Catholicism with Latin rites, but the Union). In "their" part of Poland, in Galicia the Austrians allowed the Union to prosper, and East-Galicia became a birthplace for Ukrainian nationalism.

Between the Wars the Orthodox Church in Eastern Galicia was in trouble by Polish nationalisation-politics. The Churches in the SU were persecuted, especially following 1928; many believers and many priests were killed.[167] During

---

166 Stefan Donecker: Konfessionalisierung und religiöse Begegnung im Ostseeraum, in Komlosy *Osteee* S. 91–109; Cf. Richard Meßner, Rudolf Pranzl Hg.: *Haec sacrosancta synodus*, Regensburg 2006: Pustet.
167 Nolte Glaubensgemeinschaften in *Handbuch der Geschichte Rußlands* Bd. 3,2 ; see above note 42. From the literature on religions in Soviet Times see Otto Luchterhandt: *Der Sowjetstaat und die Russisch-Orthodoxe Kirche*, Köln 1976: Wissenschaft und Politik; Christel Lane: *Christian Religion in the Soviet Union*, London 1978: Allen & Unwin; Peter J. Babris: *Silent Churches*, Arlington Heights/Ill. 1978. On the new editions of sources Ja. N. Shchapov Ed.: *Russkaja pravoslavnaja Cerkov' i kommunisticheskoe gosudarstvo*, Moskva 1996: Biblejsko-Bogoslovskij Institut Svjatogo Apostola Andreeva.

the 2nd World-War Germany had many supporters in these regions, for instance the nationalistic movement lead by Stepan Bandera. In 1944 the "Marxist" government of the USSR again forbade the Union, now also in the eastern part of Galicia. The fight between the three orthodox Churches in the Ukraine – one obedient to the Patriarchate Moscow, one bent on an autonomous Orthodox Church, and one obedient to Rome – came out into the open only after independence.[168]

How did the fight for the Ukraine influence the Western image of Russia? It does remind of king Rother – the Russians are not true to their commitments, they do not fight openly, (but via the movement in the Eastern Ukraine,[169]), and they do not give their beautiful daughter to the western suitor willingly, so that the suitor has to use tricks. But images aside: nation-building in the Ukraine was and is not possible without taking all three confessions into account. And the West should carefully take into consideration its own tradition of *ecclesia triumphans* – mistakes made by overestimating its own capacity to implement stable and durable governments in its Orthodox peripheries.

---

168 Theodore R. Weeks: Between Rome and Tsrgard, in. Robert P. Geraci, Mikhail Khodarkovsky Eds.: *Of Religion and Empire*, Ithaca etc. 2001: Cornell University Press, p. 70–91; Andreas Kappeler: *Kleine Geschichte der Ukraine* München 1994: Beck, p. 124–264; Kerstin Jobst: *Geschichte der Ukraine*, Stuttgart 2010: Reclam, especially p. 187–254; lately the Journal *Religion und Gesellschaft in Ost und West* 2015 Heft 8.

169 Despite the fact, that these movements are poised against the oligarchs, on whom Putin is relying in the Russian Federation – see *Quellenbuch* 7.57.

II.10 Orisha

The last case is the Orisha-creed.[170] Orishas are small gods or powerful angels close to natural powers like water, earth, air or fire.[171] There are more than a thousand of them in Yorubaland in Southern Nigeria and related territories in Dahome. To each orisha there is a specific music, dancing, and staging. There is one powerful god above the orishas, Olorun. In some mythology the orishas dethroned him but did not know how to run the world themselves, so that they had to call him back just for this job: run the world.

The centre of the religion is in what today is a holy wood called Osun in Nigeria, in the town of Ifá in Yorubaland. The oracle there in earlier times was transmitted purely oral, the priests knowing very many sentences or maxims. They throw 16 cowrie-shells, which are used as either yes or no according to the way the shells fall either on the top or on the mouth. That means, actually it is a dual system of information, an Aski-System. Today the sentences have been collected and are published.

Now when slaves from Africa where brought to the Americas they brought their religion along. From these in Brazil developed an own form called Candomblé using the old Yoruba-sentences in oracle. There was one difficulty though: Yoruba is a tonal language, in which – meaning of a word is connected with the tone of pronunciation; ha (high) means something quite different from ha (low). The slaves

---

170 For my quite superficial knowledge of this creed I am indebted to H.R.M. Oba Dr. Adedayo Olusino Adekoya (Ode Remo, Nigeria) and to Dr. Insa Nolte (University of Birmingham).

171 Miguel Barnet: *Afrokubanische Kulte*, German: Suhrkamp, Frankfurt 2000; Claudia Rauhut: *Santeria und ihre Globalisierung in Kuba*, Düsseldorf: Ergon 2012.

living in a Portuguese surrounding (and of course visiting Christian service every Sunday) did not keep that difference. But the sentences of their oracle are in one of the Yoruba-languages. Quite similar in Cuba, where the creed is called Santeria, In slavery the number of Orishas was diminished. To each Orisha belong specific colours, numbers, plants, sounds, rhythms, dishes and drinks. Also certain Saints are attributed. Let us take the Orisha Oshun – she may be asked for intervention by women, for fertility and love, but also is coordinated with water. In Candomblé the Catholic Saint identified with her is the virgin of Candelaria and Mary of the Immaculate Conception, in Santeria it is the Virgen de la Caridad del Cobre.

Already in Africa there are different systems of Orishas and different clans and groups taking part in it. This multitude enlarged, when the creed became global.

Up to a certain point the Orisha-Creed may be understood as a way of keeping an own identity before und during the forced living in the early capitalist *"ingenios"* – the sugar plantations/factories of the Americas. But the point is, that it does have a global carreer at the moment – from Southern Nigeria to New York, from Havanna to Berlin. Orisha also is connected with natural healing; rumors have it, that Fidel Castro still is alive, because he joined the Santeria. But it is a global belief, in 2014 The "Orisha World Peace and Healing Initiative" called for a global week "to show their support for world peace" wearing white clothes, taking ritual communion together and drumming. Organiser was Ile Orunmila Ogunike or in Anglo Saxon Lily Clement-Brown of Houston/Texas.[172]

---

172 http://www.oloshasunited.com (consulted May 11th 2015)

As all religions of course Orisha also is about money. Devotionals are sold, pictures, small chains, textiles. There are websites, one for instance with the name "Godchecker", and they ask for donations. Movies are made or proposed. In one of them beautiful African men and women stage as Orisha-superheros, it is called: "Oya: Rise of the Orishas" and shows the Orishas as "collective of charismatic deities with specialised supernatural gifts" for "Black British Cinema" You may donate to the cause.[173] Then there was a Cuban Hip-Hop-Band named Orisha and quite successful.

But what is the religious cause? Why is this old, but in its actual form with Journals and websites new creed that successful? One reason might be, that Orisha with music, dance and common meals is bringing the community, the "Gemeinschaft" really to life. But is that all? What is the role of this new creed in the global world?

---

173 http://blogs.indiewire.com/shadowandact/ (consulted May 11th 2015)

III Conclusions for Histories of the World and of the World-System

World- and Global History is dependent on editions of sources and secondary literature. Typically the production of these is organised in sub-disciplines on periods, spaces (area-studies)[174] institutions (Churches, International law, social movements) or topics (history of trade, "Umwelt", gender-relations, ideas). What is the best way for Global and World-History to draw on the research of the sub-disciplines?

There are different attempts to do that. Peter Feldbauers, Bernd Hausberger and Jean-Paul Lehners Global history is relying on a concept of "Worldregions" related to area-studies, the books are structured along periods.[175] Reinhard Sieders and Ernst Langthalers Global History is taking histories of institutions and topics as starting-points; religious history constitutes a special chapter; they are only treating modern times.[176] My own attempt in the two volumes from early modern to contemporary world-history is a combination – I start with systematic receptions of certain area-studies, histories of institutions and topics like global associations etc.; religious histories constitute own chapters.[177]

---

174 Birgit Schaebler Hg.. *Area Studies und die Welt*, Wien 2007: Mandelbaum. For the American experience see Wolf Schäfer: Reconfiguring Area Studies for the Global Age, in Arjomand *Social Theory*, p. 145–178; a German version ZWG 16.1 (2015) p. 149–184.
175 Feldbauer *Globalgeschichte* (note 22).
176 Reinhard Sieder, Ernst Langthaler Hg.: *Globalgeschichte 1800–2010*, Wien: Boehlau 2010 ; see Faschingseder (note 10).
177 Nolte *Weltgeschichte* 1–2: 14th to 20th centuries.

Alfred Kohler[178] and Jürgen Osterhammel[179] have written within smaller periods, using "centuries" for periodization, and have turned to religion following the internal structure of their narratives. Christopher A. Bayly has taken the safer side and included in his history of the long 19th century an own chapter on religious world-empires, which allow global views on the expansions of Christianity and of Islam and offers a fine map on religious centers of Hindus, Muslims, Buddhists and Christians.[180]

Walter Demel and others in their World-History mainly structure their texts along topics, not all of which are directly connected with sub-disciplines.[181] Similarly Akira Iriye and Jürgen Osterhammel in their "History of the World" invited colleagues for broad topics like modern statehood, empires, migrations, global economy, "currents" and networks,[182] of which only migrations and economy broadly follow sub-disciplines. "Religious transnationalism" is treated by Emily Rosenberg on ten pages with a broad view, but not recurring to the classical histories of Churches and religions.[183] Are less

---

178 Kohler *Welterfahrungen* (note 84) On the 16th century.
179 Osterhammel *Verwandlung* (note 3).
180 Christopher A. Bayly: *Die Geburt der modernen Welt. Eine Globalgeschichte 1780–1914* [2004] German Frankfurt: Campus, 2006; here p. 400–450, map 436 f.
181 Walter Demel, Johannes Fried, Ernst-Dieter Hehl and others eds.: *WBG Weltgeschichte*, Vol 1–6, Darmstadt: Wissenschaftliche Buchgesellschaft, 2009–2011.
182 Akira Iriye, Jürgen Osterhammel eds.: *A History of the World*, Cambridge/Mass. I only used the volume Emily S. Rosenberg Ed.: *A World Connecting. 1870–1945.*: Cambridge/Mass: Belknap Press, 2012.
183 Emily Rosenberg: Religious Transnationalism, in: Iriye *History* p. 868–878.

than 1 % of the whole text adequate for religion in a period, in which – as Neudeck recalled – at least 90 % of the people in Europe (and 99 % outside of it?) still were practising believers? Most religions of the time were global – with pilgrims going to Santiago and Lourdes, to Soloveckij[184] and Jerusalem, to Mekka and Benares? Should for instance the worldwide religious reform-movements and reformers as Jamal al-Din al-Afghani not be covered in such an overview?[185]

Of course questions of representation of certain topics in World-History will always remain. But if historians would organize their texts on world-history along the sub-disciplines they use, that would offer the possibility to give a very short introduction to it and present collections of sources, classical overviews, Journals, special encyclopaedia's etc., which would enable the reader to follow the text with more insight into its scientific status – is it an attempt to develop the own concept, but on the basis of the "state of the art"?

Within World-System-Analysis religions might be seen as subsystems with high autonomy. A couple of religions are global and some even have global institutions, from the Catholic Church with its centre in Rome, the Calvinists with their centre in Geneva, the Lutherans with their centre in Hannover, the Muslims with their central organisation of Islamic Conferences

---

184 For an introduction to this pilgrimage see Hans-Heinrich Nolte: Solovecki, in: Martin Stöber, Karl H. Schneider, Olaf Grohmann Hg.: *Insel-Reflexionen, Carl-Hans Hauptmeyer zum 60. Geburtstag*, Hannover 2008, p. 65–70.

185 See, with the focus on political contexts, Pankaj Mishra: *Au den Ruinen des Empires. Die Revolte gegen den Westen und der Wiederaufstieg Asien* [2012] German Frankfurt; S. Fischer, 2013, and more on religious contexts Christian Lekon: Ägytischer Reformislam und Säkularisierung, 1870–1935, in *ZWG* 16.1 (2015) p. 63–94.

in Jidda and the leaders of certain denominations as the Wahabites in Rhiyadh, and of course the Orisha with their spiritual centre in Ifá. For our judgement religious institutions are historical, they have beginnings and ends, but many are far longer in existence than the European World System. For their roles in the context of that eight points may be summarized:

1. Starting research close to the actors sources from religious contexts enable concrete views "from above" and "from below". These sources might set off attempts at generalisation in interdisciplinary discussions – as Weber did in his sociology of religions – and as might be done discussing contemporary religions as Orisha.
2. In many religions large wealth is collected, from the gifts of widows in medieval times to the income from devotionals and music for Orisha today. This wealth in some cases – we know about Britain, Germany and Russia – is transferred into state-expenses, industry and business.
3. The political and intellectual history of the European World System is part of a transition from an universalist and Christian Empire to secular ways of organising societies and political institutions. Despite its global success in the long 19th century the World-System may come to an end earlier, than many religions.
4. We may propose forms in the uses of religions for further research as typical, though not exclusive, for certain regions of the World-System:
   a. In the centres a use for stabilising states and as trajectories from political participation in estates to parliaments
   b. In the semi-peripheries a use for creating states capeable to organise attempts of catching up
   c. In the peripheries a use for legitimising and organising defence of sovereignty or anti-systemic movements.

6. The most successful (though not the only possible) forms of political units within the Modern World-System are Nation-states (as long as they offer the most stable conditions for economics and politics). Nation-states as a rule are constructed along with national religious institutions.
7. Religion, especially religious fundamentalism, offers possibilities for organising and legitimising anti-systemic movements: "*Widerstand*", resistance or, to borrow a fine phrase from Alf Lüdtke: "*Eigensinn*", obstinacy[186].

*

The study of religion quite often poses new questions in the common search of sociologists and historians for answers to the old question, (to quote the Orishas) how the world is run. Whether atheists, Muslims or believing Lutherans – all social scientists will find, that the historical part in the multiple process of answering this question will not work without the history of religions. In this sense I may perhaps end with St. Augustins "inquietum est cor nostrum…",[187] and finish the sentence in the way of secularised science: "our heart is restless, until we understand" (at least a little).

---

186 Lüdtke uses the term for proletarian milieus, see the collection of articles: Alf Lüdtke: *Eigen-Sinn, Fabrikalltag, Arbeitererfahrung und Politik vom Kaiserreich bis in den Faschismus*, Münster: Westfälisches Dampfboot, 2015.
187 I read Hans Urs von Balthasar Hg.: Augustinus: *Bekenntnisse*, German Frankfurt 1956 (Fischer); here Book 1, Chapter 1, article 1.

www.ingramcontent.com/pod-product-compliance
Ingram Content Group UK Ltd.
Pitfield, Milton Keynes, MK11 3LW, UK
UKHW021837140426
5217IPUK00022B/1495